first names

NELSON
Mandela

Nansubuga Nagadya Isdahl

Illustrations by Nicole Miles

Abrams Books for Young Readers

NEW YORK

The facts in *First Names: Nelson Mandela* have been carefully checked and are accurate to the best of our knowledge, but if you spot something you think may be incorrect, please let us know. Some of the passages in this book are actual quotes from Nelson and other important people. You'll be able to tell which ones they are by the style of type: *Well, I am not a saint . . .* The pronunciation guide at the back of the book will help you to read the African words and names.

Library of Congress Control Number 2021934539

ISBN 978-1-4197-5608-5

Book design by Charice Silverman

Printed and bound in U.S.A.
10 9 8 7 6 5 4 3 2 1

ABRAMS The Art of Books
195 Broadway, New York, NY 10007
abramsbooks.com

NO MORE APARTHEID

Contents

Introduction—Nelson Arrives at the Great Place

THE PLACE: The royal residence of the acting king of the Thembu people, Transkei, South Africa
THE YEAR: 1930

It was late in the afternoon, the sun was setting, and twelve-year-old Nelson was exhausted. He'd been walking up and down hills and along dirt roads with his mom, pulling his trusty tin trunk, since the crack of dawn. They were headed to his new home and hadn't talked much on the journey. They hadn't stopped either. But when they arrived at their destination—a large and noble-looking residence in the middle of a quaint village at the bottom of a green valley—and walked through the gates, his exhaustion was quickly forgotten.

Nelson couldn't believe his eyes. Sprawled out in front of him were two large rectangular houses with tin roofs and bright white walls, seven nice-looking huts, a large vegetable garden, peach and apple trees, hundreds of sheep, and even a church! (All sure signs of great wealth in rural South Africa at the time.) Nelson had never seen such a magnificent place before. It was far grander than the modest grass-roofed huts he'd lived in for most of his life.

He'd barely taken it all in when a huge Ford V8 motor car came roaring through the gate. Nelson hadn't seen many cars in his life either—back in his village of Qunu they were a rare sight. And he definitely hadn't known a single soul who actually owned a car as nice as this one.

A group of respectable elders jumped to their feet, tipped their hats, and shouted, "Hail, Jongintaba." The car door opened, and a short, stout man wearing a suit emerged.

Nelson was impressed. He knew that this man, who seemed able to command the respect of other people without saying a word, was going to be his legal guardian from now on.

Thanks to his father's friendship with Jongintaba, a new world of privilege was suddenly opening up for Nelson, and it seemed both exciting and shocking! Gone was the simple, secure life he'd lived with his mom. Gone was his chance to be crowned champion stick-fighter by his fellow herdboys. And gone were the evenings of listening to his father's tales of historic battles and heroic warriors.

Jongintaba had full command of the Thembu kingdom and **the power to change people's lives**, but he would never be king himself. He was only stepping in as regent or "acting king" until the real king, a young boy named Sabata, was old enough to take charge.

Nelson felt like he was being thrown into a river and carried off downstream with no idea where it would take him, but the Great Place was an important stepping-stone for him. He didn't know it yet, but living with Jongintaba would help him get to university, become the owner of one of the first Black law firms in Johannesburg, the leader of a movement that would help to free his people, and the first Black president of South Africa. A global symbol of courage, justice, and equality for everyone, everywhere, Nelson didn't just change his country; **he changed the world**.

But I never forgot where I came from. I was proud of my roots.

You became a hero for so many people across the globe, but your fight to free your people landed you in prison for twenty-seven years! How did you survive?

With the support of my family, friends, and fellow freedom fighters. Prison was brutal, but there were moments of true friendship and laughter.

Didn't you ever lose faith?
No. Even when things seemed impossible, I learned that just by putting one foot in front of the other slowly but surely you can reach the finish line.
But how exactly did you get to the finish line?
Well, it's a long story—we should get started!

1 Nelson Is Named

Nelson wasn't actually called Nelson when he was little. As a member of the Thembu people, he'd been named Rolihlahla. The name means tree-shaker in his local language, isiXhosa,* but it could also mean troublemaker. In his early years, though, Rolihlahla hardly caused any trouble at all.

He'd been born into the royal Thembu family on July 18, 1918.

ROLIHLAHLA EXPLAINS: MY TRIBE AND ANCESTRY
I belong to the Xhosa people of South Africa, and we have many tribes.
Mine is the Thembu tribe. My great-grandfather was once king of the Thembu people, but because of the strict rules about accession to the throne, there is no way I will ever be king!

* See Pronunciation Guide on page 146.

Each tribe belongs to a clan that is traced back to a specific ancestor.

I am a member of the royal family, but I won't be trained to rule. The plan for me is to take on my father's important role (see bottom of page).
Ngubengcuka was one of the greatest Thembu kings. He was my great-grandfather.
Here's my family tree—it skips a few generations.

Ngubengcuka

(Great house)

Ngangelizwe

Dalindyebo

Jongilizwe

Sabata

(Heir to the Thembu kingdom)

(Left house)

Inkosi Mandela

Gadla Henry Mandela

Rolihlahla (Nelson) Mandela

My dad isn't just the chief of my village, he is also adviser to the regent, Jongintaba.

Rolihlahla's father, Gadla Henry Mphakanyiswa Mandela, had **four wives and thirteen children**! In Thembu culture, it was common for a man to have more than one wife—Rolihlahla's mom, Nonqaphi Nosekeni, was his dad's third.

Gadla Henry usually only spent a week at a time with each wife, so little Rolihlahla didn't get to see him much. Then something happened that meant Rolihlahla got to see him even less.

As a village chief and royal adviser, Gadla Henry was wealthy and well respected, but he was also stubborn. When a British judge summoned him to court because of a complaint about a stray ox, Gadla Henry replied:

No, I refuse to come. I have many important things to tend to.
Oh!

The king of the Thembu tribe might have named Gadla Henry chief, but South Africa was ruled by the

British at the time. When the British issued an order, people were expected to listen. Refusing an order was shocking, and Gadla Henry had to be punished—so the judge took his title, most of his herd, and most of his land, **no questions asked**!

My father was a proud Thembu man. He didn't see why he should follow the laws of some king he'd never seen, who lived thousands of miles away.

The British had been in Africa for a long time, though, and they'd made many powerful and unfair laws:

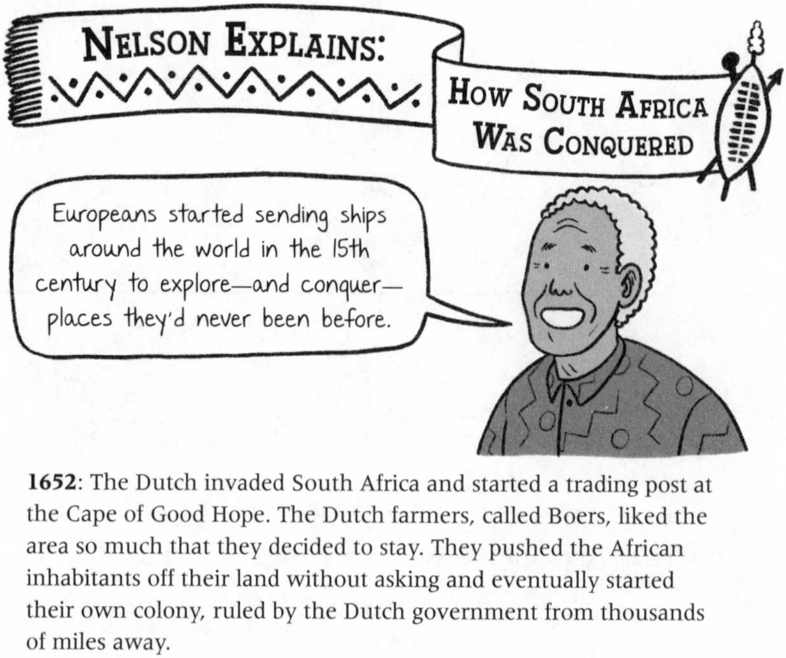

NELSON EXPLAINS:
HOW SOUTH AFRICA WAS CONQUERED
Europeans started sending ships around the world in the 15th century to explore—and conquer—places they'd never been before.

1652: The Dutch invaded South Africa and started a trading post at the Cape of Good Hope. The Dutch farmers, called Boers, liked the area so much that they decided to stay. They pushed the African inhabitants off their land without asking and eventually started their own colony, ruled by the Dutch government from thousands of miles away.

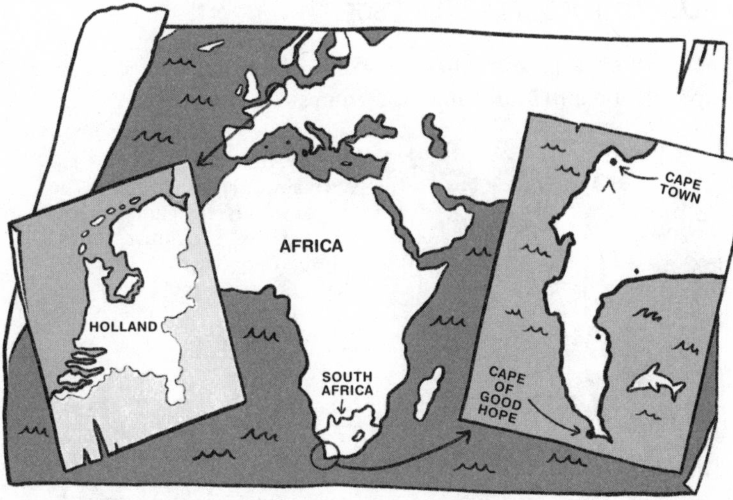

1700s to early 1900s: The Africans fought the Europeans, but the Europeans had a big advantage: guns. On the other hand, they were also fighting among themselves. The British had wrestled the Cape colony from the Dutch, and the Dutch battled to get it back again. In the end, the British won and took control of the South African colonies. When gold and diamonds were found in South Africa, the Europeans definitely didn't want to leave.

1910: The British brought four of their colonies together to create the country of South Africa. They dreamed up horrible laws that separated white and Black South Africans, leaving Black people with hardly any rights at all. Most of the land was given to white people (especially the most fertile areas)—Black people were left with the poorest parts, even though all the land had once belonged to them!

UNCOMFORTABLE NEIGHBORS

Once the Europeans settled, they divided the South African population into four main racial groups:

White people . . .
originally came from Europe. The British settlers thought they were the top dogs. The Dutch settlers (eventually called Afrikaners) hated that. They spoke their own language: Afrikaans.

Indian people . . .
came from India, some as traders, but most were enslaved by the Europeans.

Colored people . . .
were of mixed race.
("Colored" is a term still used in South Africa today. It refers to people of mixed European, African, or Asian ancestry. In other parts of the world, using "colored" to refer to a non-white person is considered offensive.)

Black people . . .
were native to the land. They were subject to the worst rules because they were seen as the biggest threat to the European colonizers. There were many more Black people than white, Colored, or Indian.

We're in charge here!

Because white people had **taken the land by force**, they had better jobs than everyone else and they were represented in government. They also made voting for other groups as difficult as possible.

A Country Life

With the family fortune gone, Rolihlahla's mom decided they should move back to her own village, Qunu, just a few miles away, where at least she'd have the support of her family and friends.

Little Rolihlahla had been a herdboy since the age of five, and here he spent endless hours in the fields watching over sheep, goats, and cows or running around with his friends.

At home, at the end of the day, his mom told traditional Xhosa fables while she prepared dinner and when Gadla was there he shared tales of fearless Xhosa warriors.

Rolihlahla **loved it** when both his parents were around. Eventually, the family grew, and Rolihlahla got three younger sisters, Baliwe, Notancu, and Makhutswana. They lived a humble but adventure-filled life. Qunu was a small village of only a few hundred people set in a green grassy valley. Life there had a gentle day-to-day rhythm with traditions that had been passed from generation to generation.

Rolihlahla Explains: Life in Qunu

We may not have much stuff, but we do have loads of playmates. In Qunu all the children are my brothers and sisters and every woman is my mother.

Most of us dress traditionally in a blanket pinned at the shoulder or waist.

Tea, coffee, and sugar are only for the wealthy.
Plenty of cattle

I have so much to do! We make toys from sticks and string, swim in freezing-cold streams, and drink milk straight from the cow.

There are two small elementary schools, a general store, and a dipping tank for the cattle.

I especially love stick-fighting and play to win, but I always try to respect my opponents.

A Window to the World

Most kids in the Western world ask their parents lots of questions. That's how they learn. But Xhosa children weren't supposed to question the decisions of any elders—including their own parents. That would have been **extremely rude**! They were expected to do as they were told and to learn by watching, listening, and then imitating the adults in their life.

Boys followed in their fathers' footsteps and girls followed in their mothers'. But when Rolihlahla's dad became friends with two brothers from a different tribe, a window into a new world opened up for the family.

George and Ben Mbekela were a bit unusual for Qunu because they followed the Christian faith that had been brought to South Africa by European missionaries in the 1800s. They'd even been educated in a Christian school. This was a pretty big deal in the 1920s because the narrow-minded government thought educating Black South Africans **wasn't really worth their time**.

The brothers even convinced Rolihlahla's mom to be baptized, so she became a Christian too. Rolihlahla's father stayed loyal to the great and all-powerful Xhosa god, Qamata.

The Mbekela brothers took a liking to Rolihlahla and talked to him when he was playing in the fields.

One day, George Mbekela came to see Rolihlahla's mom.

Your son is a really smart boy. Rolihlahla should go to school.

Rolihlahla's mom didn't say a word. She wasn't sure what to think. No one in the family had ever been educated in a British-style school before.

She waited and discussed the idea with Gadla Henry. He wasn't going to give up his traditional beliefs to become a Christian, but he understood what it could mean for his son. **He said yes right away.**

And so, at the age of seven, Rolihlahla was baptized as a Christian and sent off to school.

A "Proper" English Name

The day before Rolihlahla started school, his father took him aside and told him that he'd have to dress for his big day.

Rolihlahla felt so proud! Now he was ready to walk over the hill to the school, but he couldn't have had any idea what to expect when he got there. He was used to learning things in a different way. Up until now, his classroom had been the great outdoors. He also would've been used to speaking in his own language, isiXhosa. At school everything was taught in English . . .

Most schools in South Africa in the 1920s were founded by missionaries and based on Western-style education. The British thought African names were inferior (and they also had difficulty pronouncing them), so **each student had to be given a "proper" English name**. Rolihlahla read about Vice-Admiral Horatio Nelson—a British Royal Navy hero—later in his life and wondered if his teacher, Miss Mdingane, had named him after *that* Nelson.

Rolihlahla was better known as Nelson for the rest of his life. Even his mom changed her name because of her new religion and changed it from Nonqaphi Nosekeni to Fanny.

Heartbreak

Nelson was at home one evening when he heard a loud commotion. His father had just arrived, but when Nelson entered his mom's hut to see him, he found his dad lying on the floor having a coughing fit.

Gadla Henry stayed in the hut for days, hardly moving or speaking. Though he was very ill, Gadla Henry did manage to send for one visitor: Jongintaba. A few years earlier, Nelson's dad had recommended that Jongintaba become the regent of the Thembu kingdom, and now **he had a favor to ask** in return.

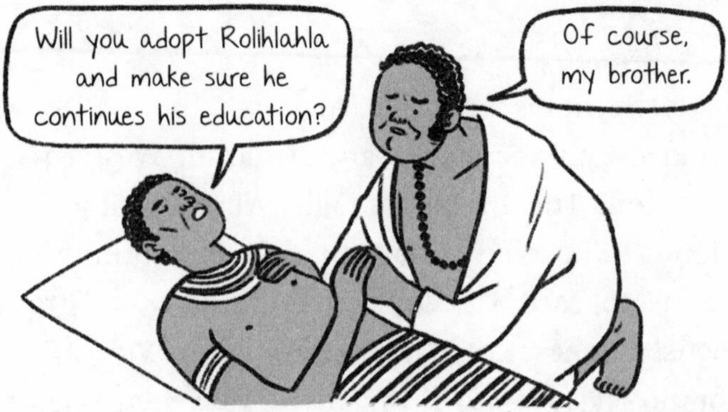

A few nights later, Gadla Henry smoked his tobacco pipe for one last time and, shortly afterward, he died.

Nelson was heartbroken. He'd always looked up to his dad and wanted to be just like him. Now he felt lost. But just as Nelson was coming to terms with his grief, his world was turned upside down once again. His mom told him he was moving away. Nelson didn't ask why he was leaving or where he was going—it wasn't his place to question his elders. He just put on a brave face, packed his few belongings, and set off early one morning with his mom.

As they walked away, Nelson took one last look back at his village and the three simple huts that had been his home. **He wondered if he'd ever see them again.**

Living with Royalty

Of course, Nelson was heading for the Great Place—with the fancy Ford V8 and his new adopted father, Jongintaba. And, once he arrived, he was rocketed into a whole new world. His mom stayed with him for a day or two before heading back to Qunu. When she left, she just gave him a tender look and said, "Be strong, son!"

She must have known that my life would never be the same again!

Nelson missed his mom and his sisters, but he quickly settled into the luxury of the Great Place. Instead of a dirt floor, Nelson's new hut had beautiful wooden floorboards. In place of his father's old pants, he got **his first brand-new outfit**.

From the day Nelson arrived, Jongintaba and his wife, Nkosikazi No-England, welcomed him into the family with wide-open arms. Nelson got along especially well with Jongintaba's two children and another boy who lived with them.

Nelson's nickname is "Grandpa," because he always looks so serious, like an old man!

Brother of two-year-old heir to the throne, Sabata

True to his promise, Jongintaba sent Nelson to school, where he had history, geography, Xhosa, and English lessons. Nelson studied hard and did well, but not without the help of his aunt Phathiwe, who inspected his homework each night.

When he wasn't at school, **Nelson's chores included ironing**! He spent hours happily and proudly pressing creases into the trousers of the regent's many suits. The Great Place was far more modern than Qunu, so it wasn't unusual to see men in suits and women in long Western-style skirts and blouses.

Soon Nelson was so comfortable in his new home that sometimes even he got into trouble. One afternoon, he snuck into the garden of Reverend Matyolo from the local church, stole some corn, roasted and ate it! Unfortunately for Nelson, a girl spotted him and reported him to the entire village.

When No-England found out, she was absolutely furious and gave Nelson a good talking-to. She and the regent never missed a Sunday in church, and stealing—from a reverend, no less!—was just about **the biggest sin** Nelson could have committed. He had disgraced the family. He felt ashamed and guilty, especially when . . .

No-England scolded me
as if I was her own child.

Nelson's favorite person at the Great Place was Justice, though their personalities were very different. Justice was outgoing; Nelson was quiet. Justice picked up new things easily; Nelson had to work hard. Justice was a risk-taker; Nelson was more cautious. But they soon became close friends. And, with his father gone, **Nelson really looked up to Justice.**

The Regent Holds Court

Beyond Nelson's own little world, life at the Great Place revolved around Jongintaba and the chieftaincy. The regent seemed to have power and influence over everything connected to it.

Whenever there was an important matter to discuss—a drought, new laws, or a dispute—a meeting was called. Thembu men (women probably weren't invited) would come from near and far—on foot, by wagon, or on horseback—and gather under an enormous tree.

Jongintaba would explain the reason for the meeting, then he wouldn't speak again until everyone else had aired their concerns and opinions. Anyone could speak, and they weren't to be interrupted.

Nelson started helping out, fetching firewood or tea for the elders. Sometimes he even managed to stuff himself with food from the great feast that was prepared for the day.

At first, he wasn't allowed to listen to the conversations. But, over time, they let him stay. And **Nelson was captivated**. The debates were lively, open, and fair. The regent didn't bark back when someone criticized him. Instead, he listened patiently without saying a word.

At the end of the meeting, Jongintaba summed up the points they'd discussed and tried to reach an agreement. If he failed, another meeting was held, and then another . . . until they figured out a solution.

As the sun set and the meeting came to a close, everyone would gather around the fire to sing traditional songs and tell stories of great ancestors. One chief told stories of life before the white people came, and the fellowship that had existed between tribes.

Nelson was fascinated, but he was also confused. Why was the history he learned on those magical nights so different from the history he was learning at school?

2 Nelson Gets Some Boots

In 1934, when Nelson was sixteen, the regent decided that it was time for him and Justice to follow an age-old Thembu custom that signaled the leap from childhood to manhood: he wanted the boys to be circumcised.

A traditional ceremony was arranged, and Justice, Nelson, and twenty-four other boys headed to two secluded huts on the banks of the Mbashe River. It felt like they were on some sort of special mission, and the boys were determined to have fun, playing games and telling stories into the night. They sang and they danced. **They even stole a pig**, butchered it, and roasted it by moonlight!

There was once a brave miner digging for gold in Johannesburg . . .
Mining in Johannesburg! How exciting!

After a few days, they headed to the river early in the morning for a cold bath—it was time.

Circumcision

In Xhosa culture, circumcision is an important ritual to prepare a boy for manhood. It involves a traditional surgeon cutting off the foreskin from the boy's most private part. At this sacred time, the boys learn about their ancestors, their family, and how to become a brave man who can serve society. Traditionally, a man could not marry or inherit his father's wealth if he was not circumcised.

Was Nelson anxious? Of course he was. He was going to have to be incredibly brave in front of a huge crowd of family, friends, and community members who had gathered to watch the ceremony. Drums sounded, and he and the boys sat on the ground to wait their turn.

An elderly man appeared from a tent and the ritual began. As the first boy was cut Nelson heard him shout, "I am a man!" as they'd all been told to do. When it was Nelson's turn, he tried not to flinch. But the pain was excruciating and he couldn't help burying his chin in his chest. Then he remembered to call out "I am a man." The hardest part was over.

After a few days' healing there was a great celebration to welcome them into society as men. Nelson was given **two cows and four sheep**—he was so proud; he'd never felt so rich in his life!

Great Expectations

Nelson passed his school exams and was soon leaving home again, for Clarkebury Boarding Institute, a secondary school 40 miles (60 km) away. Getting in to the school was such a huge achievement that another big party was thrown and Nelson received another present: his very first pair of boots.

Nelson was so over the moon that, even though the boots were already shiny, he proudly polished them up again that night.

A few days later, Nelson and the regent took off in the Ford V8 to his new school. As the scenery flew by, the regent told Nelson about the history of the school. Clarkebury had been founded on land given by his great-grandfather, King Ngubengcuka. While at the school, Nelson was expected to bring honor to his great-grandfather, to Sabata, and the entire Thembu people! It must have made Nelson nervous. He was about to enter another new world, and **everyone was expecting a lot from him**.

And it was with the weight of those great expectations on his shoulders that Nelson arrived at Clarkebury. He'd never seen a school like it before, with dormitories, classrooms, and a library! Then Nelson met the school's headmaster, Reverend Harris, and shook a white man's hand for the very first time.

No white people had ever played a real part in Nelson's life until now.

The regent explained that Nelson's role in the Thembu kingdom was to one day be **counselor to the king**. He asked that Nelson be treated with special attention. Reverend Harris agreed. All students had to work around the school grounds, but the headmaster gave Nelson a special job: tending his garden. With that sorted out, the regent handed Nelson a pound note for pocket money—a massive amount in those days—and said goodbye.

Overconfident and Underprepared

Nelson felt he was off to a great start—his pockets were heavy, he had a cushy job, and he was full of pride about his royal connections—but then he met the other students.

No trumpets blew. No one knew or even cared that I was a descendant of the illustrious Ngubengcuka!

It turned out that lots of them came from high-ranking backgrounds and some were far more sophisticated than he was. Nelson was about to learn this lesson firsthand.

The next morning, he put on his shiny new boots and confidently made his way to class. Unfortunately, his boots had other plans. This was **the first time Nelson had ever worn boots** and he stumbled and fumbled, making a terrible racket as he clomped up the stairs, then crashed into the classroom.

From the corner of his eye, Nelson saw two girls watching him, trying not to laugh.

Nelson was horrified . . . and then absolutely furious. He was determined to prove he was just as good as those girls!

Clarkebury had a very strict regime, and even the teachers feared the headmaster. But for education and sports, it was top-notch. Nelson took up tennis and football, though for him lessons were most important.

After a shaky start, worrying that he might not pass his exams, Nelson put his nose to the grindstone and flew through his program, catching up with the girls in just two years instead of the usual three!

English Life

When Nelson was nineteen, he joined Justice at an even fancier school—Healdtown, the largest African school south of the equator at the time. Healdtown felt completely different from Clarkebury. The very British headmaster, Dr. Arthur Wellington, took every opportunity to **brag about his famous relative** the Duke of Wellington, who had defeated the French emperor Napoleon in 1815.

There was a strict English-inspired schedule too:

6 a.m.: First bell
6:40 a.m.: Breakfast (dry toast and hot sugar water)
8 a.m.: Stand at attention in the courtyard as the girls arrive from their dormitories
12:45 p.m.: Break from classes for lunch: boiled porridge, sour milk, and beans
Afternoon: Study
5 p.m.: Break for exercise and dinner
7–9 p.m.: Study
9:30 p.m.: Bedtime. Lights out!

Nelson was a country boy and, like everyone in his village, he usually ate with his hands. He really struggled with British table manners, especially eating with a knife and fork. Male and female students had meals together on Sundays and Nelson, determined not to embarrass himself with his clumsy eating habits, often left the dining hall with an empty stomach!

He enjoyed the British-style education much more and even **took up boxing and long-distance running**. He got his first real taste of leadership as a student monitor, supervising other students' chores and trying to keep them out of trouble.

But it was a special performance in his final year at Healdtown that really stood out for Nelson and stirred something deep inside him. A great Xhosa poet visited the school, and Nelson and his classmates were ecstatic. His own culture had never been celebrated in a big way at school before. The poet spoke of Xhosa history and predicted something that seemed **unimaginable** at the time:

One day we Africans will be free to rule ourselves.
Seeing a Black man onstage in traditional dress felt amazing. It changed everything for me.

The effect of that speech lasted long after the performance had ended. Nelson started to wonder: **What if Africans could be free from the British?** Maybe he wasn't just Xhosa, or even South African. Maybe he was part of much larger African brotherhood.

Nelson's Big Dreams

Nelson was twenty-one by the time he finished secondary school in 1938, and he had big dreams. He'd been accepted at one of the best universities in the region—Fort Hare.

Here's what Nelson hoped the future held: he'd study to be a civil servant; then he'd build a home for his mother in Qunu, with a garden and modern furniture; and he'd support his whole family so that they could afford the things they'd been denied for so long.

But first he had to learn things like how to:

Use a toothbrush and toothpaste, instead of toothpicks and ash.
Wash with soap, instead of harsh blue detergent.
Use flushing toilets and hot-water showers, instead of buckets of cold water.
Wear pajamas.

Outside of school, Nelson taught Bible classes in neighboring villages with another student, Oliver Tambo (Nelson was sure this boy was destined for great things). He also **learned ballroom dancing**.

Usually the boys had to dance with each other, but one night they snuck out of the dormitory to a local dance hall. Students weren't allowed inside, but the boys thought they looked so sophisticated in their school suits that no one would recognize them. And it worked!

Inside, Nelson approached a girl for a dance, thinking he was the coolest cat on the dance floor . . . then he realized she was actually a professor's wife and he had to hightail it back to college.

But Nelson didn't really like to break the rules. He was even uncomfortable when other students did it.

One year, during the winter holiday, he invited his friend Paul home. Paul was well known on campus—his father had been president of the African National Congress (ANC). Nelson had heard the organization was important but didn't really know why.

In town one day, the boys were standing outside the post office when the local magistrate asked Paul to go in and buy him some stamps. It was not unusual in those days for a white man to bark orders at a Black man. **The Black man was expected to obey.** Paul, however, refused. The magistrate was furious. Nelson was shocked and felt uncomfortable, but at the same time he couldn't help admiring Paul. **A seed was planted** in Nelson's mind.

Maybe we don't have to put up with the way white people treat us after all?

An Unexpected Decision

Nelson started his second year feeling hopeful. His plan to return home, get a good job, and take care of his family seemed to be coming together. Work was going well, he was popular at university, and he'd even been nominated to join the Student Representative Council (SRC). Six members would be elected in the final term of that year.

Well, that was the plan, until college meals got in the way. The food in the dining hall was so awful that the students wanted the SRC to be granted more power to change it. When some students decided to **boycott the elections** in protest, Nelson joined them.

Unfortunately, the plan backfired. Because twenty-five students did vote, the six SRC members were elected, Nelson included. Most of the student body hadn't voted, though, so the six agreed that it hadn't been a fair election and that they should all resign.

They handed a resignation letter to the principal, Dr. Kerr. The principal was not amused. A new round of elections would take place the following day, he decided, in front of the whole school.

The same twenty-five students voted, and the same six SRC representatives were elected. The other five SRC members decided to accept the position without the extra powers the students had asked for, but Nelson found himself in a pickle. Most of the students still hadn't voted, so the election still wasn't fair. He felt he had to **resign a second time**.

Nelson went alone to tell Dr. Kerr and the principal asked him to sleep on his decision—he gave Nelson something else to think about too:

If you don't change your mind by the morning, I'll have no choice but to expel you from the university.
Gulp!

Nelson was badly shaken. He'd never had to make such an important choice in his life. Did he really want to throw away all his hard work and the honor he could bring to his family, the regent, and his tribe for a vote about the lunch menu? But the problem was, he'd already taken a stand. Maybe a bit of his dad's stubbornness was creeping in, because he felt it was morally right to stick with his decision.

After a terrible night's sleep, Nelson gave Dr. Kerr his final decision:

I will not serve on the SRC unless all students vote.

The principal hadn't expected this . . . so he threw Nelson a lifeline. He could have the whole summer to think it over. If he changed his mind and joined the SRC, he could return to Fort Hare. If he didn't, that was it . . . **no more college for Nelson, and no degree**!

He knew it could ruin his future career, but something inside Nelson wouldn't let him back down. He didn't like being forced into a decision. Nelson wanted power over his own fate.

At the end of the term, he took his exams (and passed them). Then he headed home to the Great Place with his future hanging in the balance.

3 Nelson Heads for the City

Nelson had no choice but to tell the regent the whole election story—and the small fact that he might be expelled from college. **The regent was furious** and insisted Nelson had to return to Fort Hare in the fall.

Nelson couldn't argue with an elder, so he kept quiet and went on with day-to-day life at the Great Place, running errands, looking after the herd, and messing around with his best friend and partner-in-crime, Justice.

A few weeks later, the regent called the boys to a meeting. He had two pretty big announcements to make. There was bad news:

And very bad news:

ARRANGED MARRIAGES went something like this:

Parents would look for a partner of the right social standing for their son or daughter.

Once a match was made, the groom's parents negotiated a bride price (usually involving cattle) to be paid to the bride's parents.

Celebrations were held and the families were officially joined.

Nelson had always known an arranged marriage would be in the cards for him one day, but he was a romantic at heart. He wanted to decide for himself who he'd marry. **Both boys were horrified** by the regent's plans. But the brides had already been chosen—and the bride price already paid!

Nelson knew he couldn't go through with it. But he also knew that if he didn't follow the regent's orders, he couldn't stay under the regent's roof any longer. The boys had no other option:

ESCAPE ARTISTS

The boys didn't tell anyone about their secret plan. When the regent headed off on a week-long business trip, they decided to seize the moment.

Penniless, and with one suitcase between them, Nelson and Justice took off, **selling two of the regent's oxen** in order to hire a car to get to the train station. The plan was to jump on a train to Johannesburg.

The regent must've known the boys were up to something, though. When they got to the station, the manager refused to serve them!

They drove to the next station and were able to catch a train . . . but it only took them to Queenstown, where they faced yet another challenge. They had their passes with them, but not the travel permits they needed to leave their district.

Nelson Explains: The Awful Pass Laws

For Black South Africans like me, travel was complicated and humiliating back in the 1940s.

Black men older than sixteen had to have a pass. But white people of any age could go wherever they wanted without one.

White farmers wanted us to stay in one place, to give them a steady supply of cheap workers. The pass was really supposed to make it harder for us to travel.

The pass told officials:

Where you lived
Who your chief was
If you'd paid the poll tax (for Black people only)

A white policeman, government officer, or employer could ask to see my pass at any time. If I refused, I could be arrested, fined, or even sent to jail!

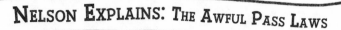

I couldn't leave my district without a pass, a permit, and a letter from my guardian.

Luckily, the boys bumped into the regent's brother, who agreed to take them to the local judge to sort out travel documents for them. They weren't exactly honest with him—the uncle had no idea they were really **on the run**!

The documents were just about ready, when the magistrate asked for one last thing . . .

I'll just call your home district to make sure you have permission to leave.
The regent happened to be in the district office as the call came through!
They do NOT have permission. Arrest them and bring them back here immediately!

The regent and the judge were fuming, but from the bit of law he'd studied at Fort Hare, Nelson knew the judge didn't have the right to arrest them. "We haven't been honest with you," he admitted, "but we haven't actually broken any laws." The judge couldn't argue with that. He just threw the boys out of his office and told them to never come back.

In the end, they got a ride the next morning with an old white lady who was driving to Johannesburg, though she took almost all their money in exchange.

Finally, finally, finally . . .
we're on our way!

The City of Gold

Nearly a whole day passed before the big city that had sparked Nelson's imagination glittered in the distance. **It was awe-inspiring.**

At home, electricity was a novelty. Here, it seemed the lights were never turned off. At home, cars were rare. Here, the streets were packed with them. There were buildings taller than any Nelson had ever seen before and huge billboards. He could hardly believe his eyes.

The old lady finally reached her daughter's house and offered Nelson and Justice a place to sleep—on the floor in the servants' quarters! But Nelson didn't mind. He was too busy imagining his future in this big city.

The next morning, at dawn, their first stop was Crown Mines, the largest gold mine in the city. The boys expected the mines to **sparkle with gold**, but instead of fancy buildings, the offices were just a jumble of **rusty old tin shacks**.

And it got worse. Hundreds of downtrodden Black workers covered in dust were running the heavy machines that squawked and squealed 24/7, while well-dressed white bosses barked orders. The noise was deafening, the work backbreaking and dangerous.

The Miserable Life of a Mineworker

Europeans had flocked to Johannesburg in the late 1800s after gold was discovered in the area. They came to seek their fortunes, bringing (and often forcing) young Black men to do the dirty work for them.

Most of the workers toiled away in deep, dark, underground shafts in scorching temperatures for up to fourteen hours a day. Serious accidents happened all the time.

As many as twenty men would live in one dingy, overcrowded room on the mine compound, with not one real toilet between them. The pay was terrible and the contracts so unfair: if a miner abandoned his job (because of the conditions), he was officially breaking the law!

Worse still, while white mine owners made their fortunes, Black families were torn apart when men had to leave them behind to work in the mines!

Being a miner must be awful!

Still, the boys were desperate for money, and as the son of the regent, Justice was lucky. He was offered a cushy clerical job, while Nelson was taken on as a watchman. The boys got free food, a place to sleep, and a small salary.

The regent's influence seemed to reach as far as Johannesburg, and many of the miners treated Justice like royalty. But then the boys boasted to another worker how they'd deceived Jongintaba and **the worker reported them**. Word was sent to the regent, who responded with a telegram saying:

SEND BOYS HOME NOW.

The boys had to flee. They were left with no jobs, nowhere to stay, and no more brilliant ideas.

While Justice reached out to a few friends and managed to find a room for himself, Nelson called a cousin, Garlick Mbekeni, who lived nearby and was happy to take him in.

Standing on His Own Two Feet

Garlick was eager to help. When Nelson explained that he wanted to study law, his cousin asked around and found the perfect contact: Walter Sisulu. Walter was an estate agent who found properties for Black Africans, and he was from the Transkei, just like

Nelson and Justice. Nelson couldn't have known it, but that day he made a friend for life.

Walter knew of a sympathetic white lawyer named Lazar Sidelsky who owned one of the largest law firms in the city—Witkin, Sidelsky and Eidelman. Even though it was practically unheard of in those days, because of racism and segregation, **the office took on Black clients**. Mr. Sidelsky hired Nelson as a clerk.

South Africa's Horrible Racial Divide

In South Africa in the 1930s, there were four Black people for every single white person, so white South Africans could only stay in power by keeping other racial groups down.

That's why they enforced such terrible laws and social customs—they wanted to keep the races separate, especially Black people:

- Very few Black people had the right to vote.
- They were forced to live on "reserves," basically the worst pieces of land in the rural areas.
- Their work opportunities were severely limited.
- Black people weren't even allowed in the same restaurants, parks, or bathrooms as white people!
- White people took the best of everything for themselves (land, jobs, schools, etc.), and gave Black people, Indigenous people, and people of color the leftovers. White people had MUCH better lives than everyone else.

So, Nelson was lucky to find a "real job" . . . and at a law office! He and the clerk he shared an office with, Gaur Radebe, were the **only Black African employees** in the entire company.

At first, Nelson worked as a messenger and filing clerk, but he gradually moved on to more serious jobs, like drawing up legal contracts. The law firm was pretty open-minded for the 1940s, so Nelson was trained well and treated kindly—most of the time.

But he was still living in a world where white people were treated better. Once Nelson was dictating some information to a white secretary when a white client walked in. The secretary was horrified. She couldn't be seen working for a Black man! She quickly took some coins out of her purse and said:

Nelson, go and buy me some shampoo.

It was humiliating for Nelson, but he did as he was told. He didn't want to make a fuss.

At night, Nelson knuckled down to study for the degree he hadn't completed at Fort Hare. That didn't leave him with much free time, but he was determined to make the most of what little he had.

Nelson's first white friend was another clerk from his office, Nat Bregman. Unlike most South Africans at the time, Nat didn't seem to care about a person's race, and the two became fast friends. When he went with Nat to a party, Nelson was shocked to find himself in the same room with people of all different races for the first time ever. He was even more shocked to discover how much fun it was.

A Few Hard Knocks

Black South Africans in Johannesburg were **forced to live in all-Black "townships"** and attend Black-only schools. Indian and Colored children had separate schools and places to live too. Eventually, Nelson moved to a township called Alexandra. It was overcrowded and neglected, but it was one of the few places in the entire country where Black South Africans could actually buy property.

Nelson found living there thrilling. The streets were alive with adventure and full of resourceful people. He rented a tin-roofed shack. It had a dirt floor, no heating, no electricity, and no running water, but to Nelson it was home.

And because Black people could own land here, I felt a sense of pride and promise. I grew to love Alexandra.

But he only earned two pounds per week—barely enough to cover his rent, transportation, food, and tuition fees. He'd try to save money by walking to work and back—six miles (9.5 km) each way—wearing the same clothes for days on end, and sometimes going without food. Even in Qunu, **he'd never felt as poor as this**!

The End of an Era

Nelson was twenty-three when the regent announced he was visiting Johannesburg and wanted to see his adopted son. The last time they'd met they hadn't exactly seen eye to eye, but to Nelson's relief this time there was no mention of the expulsion from college, the arranged marriage, or the escape to Johannesburg. Phew! Maybe the regent had actually accepted that Nelson had chosen his own path?

Four full years had passed since Jongintaba's dramatic announcement that he thought he was dying, but now the regent really did look old and weary. As it turned out, this was to be their last meeting. Sadly, a few months later, Jongintaba died.

And I never told him how grateful I was for his support. Where would I be now without him?

While Justice decided to face up to his responsibilities and stay at the Great Place to take on the regent's role, Nelson realized he would **never play a part in the Thembu kingship**. His world was in Johannesburg now. Everything he'd seen there—the different people, cultures, and beliefs—had shifted his outlook on life. Racism left so many people badly off. Maybe, by staying there, he could help to change things.

4 Nelson Joins the Fight

Nelson finally got his bachelor of arts degree at the end of 1942, and in January 1943 he enrolled at the University of the Witwatersrand (aka Wits) to begin studying for an LLB, or a bachelor of law. With an LLB, he could formally train as a lawyer, then he'd **really be able to help people** and earn good money at the same time.

Still plugging away in the law office, Nelson often had long chats about politics with his good friend and office mate, Gaur Radebe. It turned out that Gaur was an important man in the African community and he belonged to that organization Nelson kept hearing about: the ANC.

The ANC

Founded in 1912, the African National Congress was the oldest national African organization in South Africa. It was set up to bring Black people together to try to change the laws that took away their rights and freedoms.

Gaur had a reputation as a bit of a troublemaker in the law office, but Nelson found him fascinating. He was totally committed to the fight for freedom and happy to take Nelson under his wing.

Then, in August 1943, when Nelson was twenty-five, he finally got the chance to put some of what he'd learned from Gaur into action. A bus company in Alexandra was planning to raise its fares **from fourpence to five**. That might not sound like much, but most citizens of Alexandra simply couldn't afford it. In protest, they refused to use the buses until the bus company reinstated the old price.

Nelson took to the streets with Gaur and 10,000 Black South Africans. It was his first ever protest and he was very excited.

He could hardly believe it when, after nine days of empty buses, **the bus company gave in**! The fare went back down to fourpence. Seeing that protests could stop people from suffering, Nelson wanted to get even more involved.

Tram Trouble

Meanwhile, studying at Wits, Nelson was meeting young freedom fighters of all races who shared his conviction about changing South Africa.

He quickly made friends with four Indian students and the five of them would study, talk, and dance into the early hours of the morning.

Indians in South Africa weren't much better off than Black people at that time, but different rules applied to different groups. For example:

- Colored, Indian, and white workers were allowed to form trade unions. Black workers were not.
- Black and Indian people were forced to live in specific areas.
- Women were even worse off—only white women were allowed to vote.

One day, Nelson and two of his friends, Ismail and JN, jumped on a tram in a hurry to get back to Ismail's apartment. The conductor wasn't happy. He curtly told Ismail and JN that their "friend" (Nelson) couldn't ride with them. Ismail and JN were so furious, they shouted at the conductor.

The conductor couldn't believe his ears. By law, Indian people were allowed to travel by tram, but Black people weren't—so the conductor called the police. The next thing they knew, the boys were at the police station being charged!

Luckily, a lecturer from Wits named Bram Fischer agreed to defend them. Bram came from an important Afrikaner family, and when the boys showed up with him by their side, the judge promptly dropped all charges.

This could have been MUCH worse! Most Black people wouldn't be so lucky.

The Winds of Change

Change was stirring in the 1940s. The Second World War was raging, and all over the world, people were calling for freedom, justice, and human rights. Black South Africans were **starting to fight back**.

Anger had been brewing in Nelson too. He didn't know exactly when it had started, but he knew it hadn't happened overnight. Maybe it was those history lessons, the travel restrictions, the humiliating incident on the tram. Whatever the reason, Nelson had had enough. He didn't just want freedom for himself; he wanted freedom for all South Africans. There was one organization that might have the answers he needed. Nelson decided it was **high time he joined the ANC**!

He was a bit nervous at first. But his friends Gaur and Walter Sisulu (who'd gotten him his legal job) seemed so full of confidence. They could deliver rousing speeches to large crowds and they were so sure of their opinions. Nelson, on the other hand, was still trying to figure out what he truly believed.

However, it wasn't long before he started to make an impact. In 1944, Nelson and a few other young ANC members came up with a bold plan to get things moving in the organization:

- They formed a Youth League.

We wanted to light a fire under the feet of older members and really make things happen.

- They wrote a manifesto that explained what they wanted.

YOUTH LEAGUE MANIFESTO
We believe that the national liberation of Africans will be achieved by Africans themselves.

- They started plotting a major national campaign.

We knew changes could only happen if thousands of people showed their support.

As Nelson's involvement in the ANC grew, he spent more and more time with Walter and his wife, Albertina. Their home was warm and inviting, filled with lively discussion and interesting people, including **one special young woman** who caught Nelson's eye.

Family Life

Evelyn Mase was pretty and quiet. She came from the Transkei region, like Nelson. She was also Walter's cousin and was studying to be a nurse with Albertina. The whole family seemed to adore her.

Nelson didn't waste any time asking her out, and before long, the two had fallen in love. A few months later, they were married.

With hardly any money between them, instead of the traditional wedding ceremony and massive feast for hundreds of guests, Nelson and Evelyn opted for a small ceremony in Johannesburg and quickly moved on to something much more practical: finding a place to live.

They eventually rented their very own house in 1946 in the township of Orlando West in Soweto. It was about **the size of a shoebox**! Built on a dirt road, it had no electricity and the toilet was a bucket in the back yard, but it was Nelson's very first family home and he was as proud as punch.

Later that year, Nelson and Evelyn welcomed their first child into the family—a son, named Madiba Thembekile, or Thembi for short.

Nelson loved family life and was delighted to spend as much time with Thembi as he could.

Thembi soon had a baby sister, Makaziwe. Nelson and Evelyn had hardly any money and no fancy belongings, but they were a happy little family . . . until **tragedy struck**.

Makaziwe was a sickly baby, and, when she was just nine months old, she died. Nelson was devastated. He stayed strong for Evelyn, but tried to heal his own grief by throwing himself heart and soul into the ANC.

He was elected as a leader of his local branch in 1947, and was soon pouring his blood, sweat, and tears into the job.

A Devastating Blow

ANC meetings often ran into the night, and on May 26, 1948 Nelson; his good friend from Fort Hare, Oliver Tambo; and a few other ANC members were involved in a long discussion.

Elections were taking place that day, and citizens across the country would be voting for a new leader of South Africa. Mainly white citizens, of course, since **hardly any** Black, Indian, or Colored people were allowed to vote.

There were only two parties in the running, but Nelson was pretty sure the ruling United Party would win.

The United Party
Made up of English-speaking Afrikaners and Colored people. They had supported Great Britain and the Allies in the Second World War, which had ended just three years earlier. They had very racist policies, but they weren't as bad as . . .

The National Party
Mostly made up of Afrikaans-speaking Afrikaners, with Dutch roots. They had supported Nazi Germany during the Second World War and thought that only white people should have power, and that Black people should be at the very bottom of the heap.

Nelson's meeting didn't finish until dawn. Bleary-eyed and exhausted, but eager to find out the election result, Nelson searched for a newspaper:

THE RAND DAILY MAIL
The Nationalists Triumph!

He was in total shock. This was the first time in the country's history that an Afrikaners-only party had ever been in charge of the government, and their plan for the country was based on a **hideous idea** called apartheid.

Nelson Explains: Apartheid

"Apartheid" literally means "apartness" in Afrikaans. It legalized the awful system that had kept Black people below white for centuries.

The whole horrible idea behind apartheid was that white people were better than African, Colored, and Indian people (see page 10). It was meant to keep white people in charge forever.

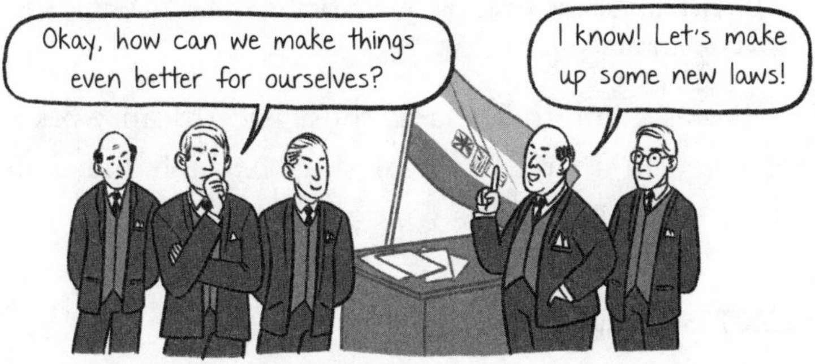

Okay, how can we make things even better for ourselves?
I know! Let's make up some new laws!

As soon as the Nationalist Party took the reins, they passed more awful, racist laws. Three of the worst ones were:

- **Every citizen who was not European had to be classified by their race.**
- **People from different races weren't allowed to marry one another.**

- **All races were forced to live, work, and buy property in specific areas—which really meant that Black, Indian, and Colored people were not allowed to live in the nicer parts of the country.**

In the past, white people had taken land only by force. Now they could take it by law too . . .

Once the horrifying news sank in, Nelson and the rest of the ANC knew they had to plan something drastic. Up until now, they'd always pushed for change politely, according to the law. But these laws were so ridiculous, they were going to have to change their strategy.

They agreed to:

- **Spread the word about their mission by going out and speaking to people across the country.**
- **Organize massive protests—national boycotts, strikes, stay-at-homes, and demonstrations.**

It was going to be dangerous. An African worker involved in a strike risked losing their job and their right to stay in the area where they lived!

Protest Day

Other groups wanted to fight apartheid too, and on May 1, 1950, a few of them got together for a big national protest. They called it Freedom Day. The idea was for people of all races across the country to not go to work to protest their loss of freedom.

Nelson and Walter went along to see what was happening. In a township south of Johannesburg, they watched from the sidelines as a well-organized group of protesters marched peacefully through the streets.

But **the police were out in force** too, with guns and batons. Suddenly they started knocking protesters to the ground. Then, before Walter and Nelson could think what to do, **bullets started flying** in their direction. The police had opened fire! Nelson and Walter dived for safety in a nearby building as the sound of gunfire pierced the air.

What started as a peaceful demonstration turned into a tragedy. **Eighteen Africans died** that day, and many others were wounded. A few weeks later, the government hit back with an even harsher law that made anything that even looked like a protest illegal.

By now, Nelson had become a high-level ANC leader. He was soon planning a protest against those eighteen senseless deaths and that awful new law. The Indian Congress and South African Communist Party (who'd been working closely with the ANC on workers' rights) agreed to join in, and the National Day of Protest was set to take place on June 26, 1950.

While Walter crisscrossed the country convincing local leaders to make sure people didn't go to work that day, Nelson took charge of the ANC headquarters, which were abuzz with activity.

This was the first time the ANC had organized a national, political, stay-at-home strike and with hardly any time to do everything Nelson wasn't sure they'd pull it off.

But on the day of the protest, across the country, **thousands of Black workers** did stay at home and many Black businesses did not open. The ANC made national headlines—they were sending a message to the government that they would not back down.

Nelson found the whole experience nerve-wracking but exciting. Organizing a huge national campaign was practically a 24/7 job, though, and over the past few weeks he'd hardly seen his family. Evelyn was not pleased!

Daddy's Never Home

In the middle of feverishly organizing protesters for the march, Nelson had managed to hightail it to a nearby hospital, arriving just in time for the birth of his second son, Makgatho Lewanika. But he couldn't stick around long. After a brief cuddle with the newborn, he rushed back to campaign headquarters.

In fact, Evelyn wasn't interested in politics, period. She was a devout Christian and thought Nelson could be doing far better things with his time. With his long hours at the office, he seemed about as useful as a ghost. The children noticed too.

One day, little Thembi asked Evelyn where his daddy lived. The truth was, Nelson was so wrapped up in his ANC work, **his family was starting to suffer**. But this was only the beginning . . .

5 Nelson Stirs Things Up

Not many Black South Africans owned cars in the 1950s, but that didn't stop Nelson from passing his driving test at the age of thirty-three. He wasn't planning any family day trips, though. A driver's license came in handy for a freedom fighter, and soon Nelson was the official driver for the local ANC. The whole organization was gearing up for action, and there were messages to deliver all over the country.

So, when the ANC needed an important letter signing by their president, Dr. Moroka, Nelson was tasked with delivering it. The letter would be sent to the prime minister of South Africa, demanding that he throw out six of the worst apartheid laws—which **made it even harder** for Black people to vote, travel, meet, or live freely.

With the letter in hand, Nelson hopped into his colossal Oldsmobile and started the 250-mile (400-km) journey to Dr. Moroka's home. He raised a few eyebrows.

Nelson loved driving through the countryside, but he had to be extra careful on the road. He was heading to the Orange Free State, where racial tensions were particularly high.

About 120 miles (193 km) south of Johannesburg, two young white boys on bicycles pulled out in front of him. Nelson's driving was still a little shaky, and when one of the boys turned suddenly, he couldn't brake fast enough and—*WHACK*—they crashed! **This was a disaster.**

Nelson got out of his car to help the boy up, just as a white truck driver appeared, yelling, "Don't you lay a finger on him, mister."

The boy wasn't hurt, but a white police officer was quickly on the scene, narrowing his eyes at Nelson as he searched the car, then threatened him with a night in jail.

Nelson was defenseless because of the color of his skin. The police kept him for hours. It was dark by the time he was released.

Back on the road again, Nelson drove through the night, but early the next morning, his car came to an abrupt stop. He'd run out of gas in the middle of nowhere!

He asked to buy some at a nearby farmhouse, but a white woman told him, "I'm not giving any gas to *you*," and closed the door in his face. Walking miles farther, to the next farm, Nelson tried a different strategy.

Can you spare some gas for my baas?

Baas is the Afrikaans word for "boss" or "master." Nelson **hated having to pretend** he had one, it was exactly the kind of thing he was fighting against, but it showed the farmer that he knew his place. This time, he got the gas.

Nelson finally made his way to Dr. Moroka's home, and with his mission accomplished, the journey home went smoothly. Back in Johannesburg, however, things were heating up.

The Defiers

When the ANC officially made its demand to the government for the laws to be dropped by February 29, 1952, the prime minister curtly replied:

We white people have a right to keep ourselves separate. Any African and Indian leaders trying to defy our laws will be stopped in their tracks!

Nelson and the ANC leaders felt they only had one option now: "civil disobedience"—which meant people would peacefully refuse to obey laws. They began planning a nationwide campaign.

The Disobedience Campaign

It was for a good reason: They were fighting for equal rights for everyone under the law!

It brought people together. African, Indian, and Colored people were all involved.

It was non-violent. The ANC planned strikes, demonstrations, and sit-ins. However badly the authorities behaved, the volunteers would always stay calm.

It was risky. All volunteers had to be prepared to be arrested.

It was disciplined. The police were informed of plans in advance so that the arrests could take place as peacefully as possible.

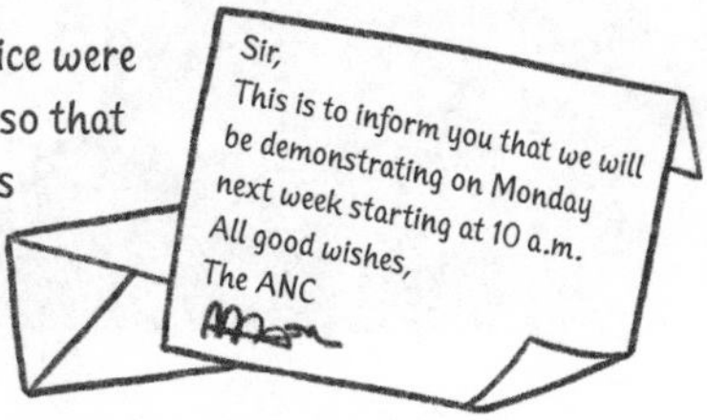
Sir,
This is to inform you that we will be demonstrating on Monday next week starting at 10 a.m.
All good wishes,
The ANC

It was well organized:

Stage 1: A few well-trained volunteers would break some laws. It wouldn't be difficult. All they had to do was:

- Enter "whites-only" areas without permits.
- Use "whites-only" facilities, such as bathrooms.

WHITES ONLY
I only went to the bathroom.

- Stay in town after a curfew that only applied to Black people.

Stage 2: Across the country people would refuse to go to work, take buses, etc.

As one of the main organizers of the campaign, Nelson drove all over the country getting ANC branches up to speed, recruiting volunteers, and raising money. At one rally just before the campaign started, he made a speech in front **10,000 people**—the largest crowd he'd ever addressed:

The Defiance Campaign will be the most powerful action ever undertaken by the oppressed masses in South Africa.

It was exciting to be involved, but it was scary too. If anything went wrong, thousands of protesters could be **risking their lives**.

In the early hours of June 26, 1952, thirty-three volunteers marched into the railway station at Port Elizabeth through the "whites-only" entrance, singing freedom songs. The police were waiting and the protesters were promptly marched back out again in handcuffs.

In Johannesburg that same evening, Nelson, Oliver, and other members of the action committee had a planning meeting. It finished just after midnight, and, as everyone left, Nelson and a friend got caught up in a protest march against the curfew that said Black people couldn't be out after 11 p.m. Nelson was exhausted but . . .

According to apartheid, Nelson was breaking the law **just by being on the street**. He'd expected to be arrested at some point, but not this soon. The campaign had only just started!

In the end, Nelson spent two days in jail. He was released, the campaign carried on, and after five months of protesting, it was **a huge success**! The specific laws the ANC had been protesting against hadn't been overturned—they'd known that was a long shot—but:

- The membership of the ANC skyrocketed from about 20,000 to 100,000.
- There hadn't been a single act of violence on the side of the protesters.
- 8,500 people—from doctors and factory workers to teachers and students—stood up to the government over the next few months.

And the government noticed. They didn't like the success of the Defiance Campaign and they started to see the ANC as a serious threat. They especially disliked the way Black and Indian people seemed to be getting closer.

So the government resorted to their usual tactics. They cracked down even harder . . .

In July, two months after the Defiance Campaign started, Nelson and twenty-one others were **arrested again** and charged with violation of the Suppression of Communism Act.

Communism in Apartheid South Africa

To most people, "communism" means a system where all citizens share the wealth that they create. But it meant something completely different under apartheid in 1950s South Africa. According to the Suppression of Communism Act, communism meant encouraging disorder or disturbance of any kind, so any disturbance was regarded as an act of communism, and people causing it could be arrested or placed under a banning order.

A "ban" meant you could only talk to certain people, you'd have to report to the police every week, you weren't allowed to speak in public, and you couldn't travel.

They were tried in September and found guilty in December. The judge showed some mercy, though: their sentence (nine months in prison with hard labor) was suspended for two years, which meant they wouldn't have to go to prison unless they committed another crime during those two years. Nelson also got a banning order. He was banned from any meetings or gatherings for **six months** and couldn't leave Johannesburg. There'd be no more driving for a while. The ban was so serious, he couldn't even go to his own son's birthday party.

Then, the government passed even more horrendous laws that said they could:

- **Bring in a military government (martial law) at any time.**
- **Imprison people without putting them on trial.**
- **Use corporal punishment, like caning or flogging, on protesters.**

Things were getting worse and worse.

First Choice and Last Resort

Aside from running around the country organizing freedom campaigns and being arrested, Nelson still had an actual job to go to. He was now able to draw up court papers, interview witnesses, and do other kinds of legal work, but he couldn't take a case to court yet. He wasn't a fully qualified lawyer.

Evelyn was still working as a nurse, but even by combining both their salaries, they could barely make ends meet. After failing the exams for his LLB degree at Wits more than once (which was hardly surprising, considering everything he had going on), Nelson found a solution. He held off on getting his full degree (for now), but made sure he passed the exam that qualified him to try cases in court. That way, he could at least start making some money.

By now, Nelson had become great friends with Oliver Tambo, who was also a practicing lawyer. He asked Oliver to join him in their own practice, which would charge a fair price to Black clients (unlike white law firms) and in late 1952 the pair opened **the only Black law firm** in South Africa at the time.

They were absolutely swamped with cases and practically had to climb over hopeful clients to get to their office in the mornings.

It's no wonder they were so popular! Africans were

desperate for legal help because they could be arrested for mind-bogglingly ridiculous crimes, such as:

- Riding on a "whites-only" bus.
- Using a "whites-only" drinking fountain.
- Walking on a "whites-only" beach.
- Not having a passbook.
- Living in the wrong place or having no place to live at all.

While Oliver did most of the office work, Nelson spent more time in court, sometimes causing quite a stir. It wasn't just that he was a Black lawyer (which you didn't see too often at that time), or a sharp dresser (with his tailored suits), or an imposing figure (he stood just over six feet tall). **Nelson had a flair for the dramatic.**

He loved cross-examinations and took great delight in entertaining the crowds that often turned up to watch the show. Once, when a maid was accused of stealing her boss's clothes, he shocked the court by holding up some of her mistress's underwear as evidence.

But Nelson wasn't treated any better in court than he was on the street. Some white witnesses **refused to answer his questions**.

Mandela and Tambo filled a gap that had existed for ordinary Africans for decades. So many people had been turned away by other law offices or cheated by the system. Now, Nelson could finally help. This was why he'd wanted to become a lawyer in the first place.

Rocky Road

In 1953, Evelyn gave birth to a baby girl, Makaziwe, named after the daughter they'd lost six years earlier. But things weren't going well between Evelyn and Nelson. The two had different views on religion and raising children. Evelyn had even asked Nelson to choose between her and the ANC. But the fight for freedom in South Africa was Nelson's life's work. He couldn't give it up. They didn't go their separate ways right away, but **the end of the road was near**.

Nelson was troubled by his marriage problems but he didn't have much time to think about them.

THE CONGRESS OF THE PEOPLE

In June 1955, the ANC organized the Congress of the People to bring together all South Africans, regardless of race or color.

NELSON EXPLAINS: THE CONGRESS OF THE PEOPLE
The plan was to draw up a Freedom Charter for the democratic South Africa of the future. Everyone was invited to make suggestions, and ideas came in from across the country.
Most popular demand
"One man one vote."
"One man one vote."
"One man one vote."
"One man one vote."

People of all races were welcomed, and on June 25 and 26, more than 3,000 delegates met to approve the final document, while the police hung around menacingly.

The document described what was needed for a free and democratic South Africa:

THE PEOPLE SHALL GOVERN!
ALL NATIONAL GROUPS SHALL HAVE EQUAL RIGHTS!
THE PEOPLE SHALL SHARE IN THE COUNTRY'S WEALTH!
THE LAND SHALL BE SHARED AMONG THOSE WHO WORK IT!
It described the future hopes and dreams of the people.

Surprise, surprise, the government wasn't impressed. To them, the convention smelled like treason, and just as it was ending, **the police stormed the stage**, snatching pictures and documents, taking names and addresses. They collected enough information so that they could deal a crushing blow to Nelson and the ANC leaders at some point in the future.

6 Nelson Goes on Trial

In September 1955, when he was thirty-seven years old, the bans that had kept Nelson in Johannesburg for two long years expired at last. He could finally travel again, and the first place he longed to visit was his childhood home with its green rolling hills.

He wanted to see his mom and sort out some Mandela family matters, but he also had some secret ANC business to attend to while he was there.

The night before Nelson was set to leave, two-year-old Makaziwe suddenly asked:

Can I come too, Daddy?
Sorry, Makaziwe.

It wouldn't have been safe to take her, of course, but Nelson was **wracked with guilt**—he knew he hadn't been spending enough time with his children, and suddenly the trip didn't seem exciting anymore. He put Makaziwe back to bed, then, at just after midnight, he hopped in his car.

NELSON'S ROAD TRIP DIARY
DAILY NEWS
Johannesburg
Durban
The Great Place
Qunu
Cape Town
On the way to Durban for secret meetings with ANC members.
Back in Qunu with my dear old mom.
My boy!
At the Great Place, full of excitement, I honked my horn . . . in the middle of the night. Oops!
What's that noise?
Help! What's happening?
On the way to Cape Town, caught my first glimpse of wild elephants and baboons!
Met ANC leaders and escaped a police raid on the offices of a liberal newspaper. Worrying!
A few weeks later, home in time for dinner.

Nelson had taken his vacation just in the nick of time. In March 1956, after six months of freedom, for no good reason, he was slapped with another ban. It meant he couldn't leave Johannesburg for **five whole years**!

Nelson was determined not to be defeated. Why should the government decide where he could go or who he could meet? But then things got worse . . .

High Treason

In the early hours of December 5, 1956, Nelson and his family were woken abruptly by a loud knock. Nelson dressed quickly, opened the door, and found **three policemen staring at him**.

They handed him a search warrant and began to ransack his house, looking for evidence against him.

Nelson tried to reassure his frightened kids as drawers and cabinets and closets were flung open. And after about an hour of upheaval, one police officer calmly said, "Mandela, you are under arrest. Come with us." Nelson read the warrant and couldn't believe his eyes. The charge against him was high treason!

According to South African law, anyone who tried to disturb, damage, or endanger the independence or safety of the state was guilty of high treason.

Nelson was being accused of trying to overthrow the government, and **the punishment for that was death**! With no further explanation, he was taken to prison as his terrified family looked on.

THE BIG SWOOP

It turned out the police had gone to every corner of the country, storming homes and offices, and arresting any senior anti-apartheid leaders who'd had a hand in planning the previous year's Congress of the People. So, when Nelson arrived at the prison, several of his ANC colleagues were already there, and over the next few hours, more and more trickled in.

The government had made one of its biggest swoops yet. Altogether, 156 people were arrested—105 African, 21 Indian, 23 white, and 7 Colored people—including almost all the top leaders of the ANC! And they were all charged with high treason.

Over the next two weeks, Nelson and his colleagues were confined to the Johannesburg Prison on a hill in the middle of the city. It was nicknamed The Fort. Inside, Nelson and his colleagues were treated like animals.

They were ordered to strip completely naked for a doctor's inspection . . .

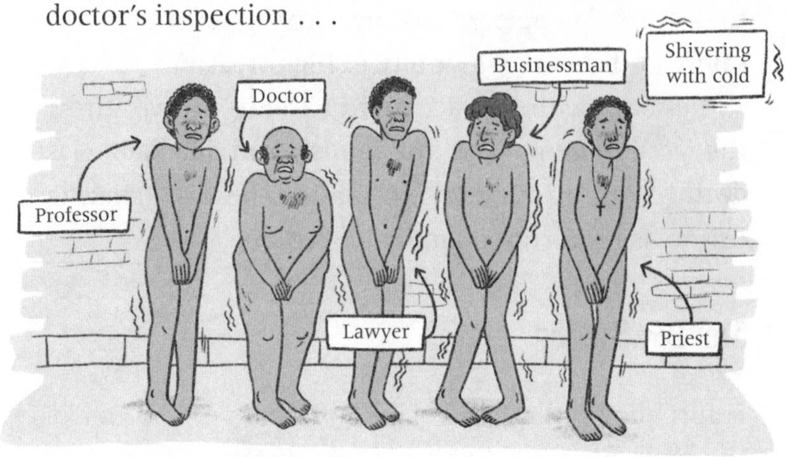

All 156 of them were held in two large cells . . .

The conditions were awful, but the one small upside was that they were all together. And no one could say that this big gathering of freedom fighters was illegal!

Before long, they'd cobbled together a program of activities that included physical training and history and political lectures! They'd sing freedom songs too, at the tops of their lungs, to keep their spirits up.

Meanwhile, outside The Fort, **people were horrified by the arrests**! Protest meetings and demonstrations were held across the country—and all over the world, in fact. People everywhere were outraged by how the South African government was treating its own citizens.

The government, however, would not be stopped. They hoped the trial would go to the Supreme Court—the highest court in the land—but first there had to be a long pre-trial to make sure there was enough evidence to convict their prisoners.

In the end, anyone found guilty could receive one of the most extreme punishments—**death by hanging**.

A Bit of a Circus

The men spent two weeks at The Fort, before attending the pre-trial in the Drill Hall. It was more like a circus. The prisoners arrived in police vans with armed guards and were greeted by hundreds of armed police.

The government must have been terrified of us!

Furious Black South Africans turned up in the thousands to surround the hall and bellow freedom songs—the case had to be stopped three times because of the noise.

Inside, the accused were forced to **sit inside an enormous six-foot wire cage** that made it impossible for them to even talk to their lawyers, though eventually they got it taken down.

It took the government prosecutors a full two days just to read the charges. And then, on the last day of the pre-trial, Nelson and the others were released on bail. The case was paused and set to begin again the following month, in January 1957.

No Place Like Home

Meanwhile, there was a surprise waiting for Nelson when he got home, and it wasn't a welcoming party. **Evelyn had finally had enough.** She'd packed up her belongings (even the curtains!) and moved out, taking the children with her. The house was empty.

Nelson admired Evelyn—she was a wonderful mom—but they'd been moving in different directions. He was crushed by the split, but it was the children—Thembi, Makgatho, and Makaziwe—who were deeply wounded by their parents' separation.

But right now, Nelson's life was on the line. The pre-trial started again and dragged on for a full year, while government lawyers examined a mind-boggling 8,000 pages of testimony and 12,000 exhibits. Then suddenly, the lawyers decided to drop charges against some of the accused. Oliver Tambo was freed! But Nelson wasn't. He would have to go on to the full treason trial. But for the moment, at least, he was allowed out on bail, and determined to make the most of his freedom.

Jailbird to Lovebird

One ordinary afternoon, Nelson was driving with a friend past a well-known hospital for Black people in Johannesburg when he noticed a young woman waiting for a bus. When he turned to look, she had disappeared, but the image of her lovely face stayed in his mind.

Imagine Nelson's delight when, a few weeks later, he strolled into his office and found the young woman sitting there talking to Oliver. Her name was Nomzamo Winifred Madikizela. She had just finished college and was starting at the hospital as its **first-ever Black female social worker**.

Nelson was so spellbound by Winnie that he barely took note of her legal problem. He was much more interested in asking her out. Yes, Nelson's first marriage had recently fallen apart and, yes, he lived a dangerous life as a freedom fighter. But Winnie was already active in the struggle and understood his motivation: **they shared the same dream**.

When his divorce was finalized, Nelson didn't actually ask Winnie to marry him, he just suggested that she should tell her parents she was getting married and be fitted for a wedding dress. Winnie didn't argue, and on June 14, 1958, she threw all caution to the wind and officially became Mrs. Mandela.

With the trial and the travel bans, **Nelson needed special permission** just to leave Johannesburg to get to his own wedding in the Transkei. Celebrations went on into the night, with singing, dancing, and speechmaking—watched over by a few unwelcome guests . . .

In his speech, Winnie's father made it clear that he wasn't optimistic about the couple's future. Nelson was a "jailbird" and already married to "the struggle," he said. But he wished his daughter well and encouraged her to stay on the path that Nelson had started.

With Winnie by my side, I felt I could cope with anything.

Nelson was thirty-nine and Winnie was just twenty-two. She probably had no idea what marrying a freedom fighter would entail:

Nelson Explains: What It Takes to Be a Freedom Fighter

Being a freedom fighter isn't as exciting as it sounds. Planning secret trips and tricking the police can be thrilling, but the hardships are not for the faint-hearted.

1. The government might harass you, ban you, or fling you into jail at a moment's notice. Worse still, they might harass and bully your family.

2. You'll have to make heart-wrenching decisions, like leaving your loved ones behind and not knowing if you'll ever see them again.

3. You might live your whole life on the run. You could be exiled to a foreign country. Or end up completely isolated in the country that you love.

4. You will never be rich—freedom fighters aren't in it for the money.

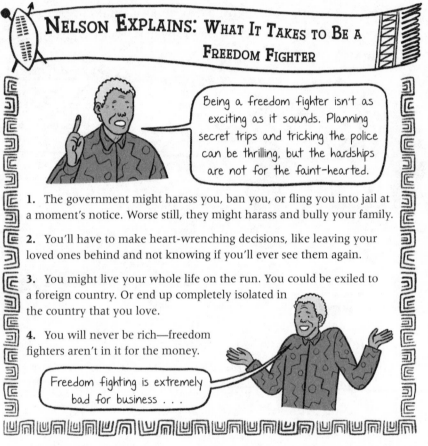

Freedom fighting is extremely bad for business . . .

Because of the pre-trial, Nelson and Winnie didn't have a honeymoon. They happily welcomed their first child, Zenani, into the world on February 4, 1959, but Nelson was at the trial instead of the birth.

From Boom to Bust

As the pre-trial dragged on into its second year, the once-bustling Mandela and Tambo law office wasn't doing so great. With Nelson away so often, clients stopped coming, and things got worse once the actual trial began. Nelson and Winnie had been surviving on Winnie's meager salary.

On August 3, 1959, nearly three whole years after Nelson's arrest, the trial finally started, 36 miles (58 km) and an uncomfortable **two-hour bus journey away**, in Pretoria. For many of the men, it was impossible to carry on working.

Nelson and the rest of the defendants—by now there were just thirty of them—pleaded not guilty. And then waited as the government put their case together. In the first two months alone, they worked their way through:

- 2,000 documents.
- 210 witnesses—lots of them were detectives who freely admitted that they'd hidden in closets, under beds, and done whatever they could to get information against the ANC.

I was just doing my duty.

Nelson and the others would have a chance to defend themselves later, but for now they had to listen. The case was slow-moving and depressing, but there was one bright point each day: the homemade spicy Indian lunch cooked by the kind-hearted wife of a fellow freedom fighter.

After seven long months, the government wrapped up their case for the prosecution, and following a short break, Nelson's lawyers would have their turn in defense. They were in for another long haul, and the Mandela and Tambo law office **just couldn't carry on**. It was finally forced to close its doors for good.

A State of Emergency

Meanwhile, outside of the trial, the struggle was still going on. Just as Nelson and the rest of the ANC leaders were gearing up to start their defense, tragedy struck.

Another African organization, the Pan-African Congress (PAC), had planned a protest against the hated apartheid laws, especially the passbook (see page 39).

On March 21, 1960, Black Africans took action across the country, and in a small township called Sharpeville, 40 miles (64 km) south of Johannesburg, several thousand Black Africans marched toward the police station. They were unarmed, but didn't have their passbooks, so they were fully prepared to be arrested.

Inside the station only seventy-five police were on duty, not nearly enough to deal with the crowd, and they panicked. Without warning, as the people approached, **the police suddenly opened fire**, wounding and killing innocent protesters as they ran for cover.

When the dust had settled, the statistics of the Sharpeville Massacre were grim:

- More than 700 shots had been fired into the crowd by the police.
- Over 150 people had been wounded.
- 69 unarmed Black Africans had died, most of them shot in the back as they were running away.

The police had been ruthless before, but this was horrific. Photos from Sharpeville made front-page headlines around the world. And, **around the world, people took notice** and began shouting out against the dreadful apartheid government.

The ANC felt they had to do something, so they called for a national day of mourning and a national day of protest. Nelson and his colleagues burned their passbooks in front of hundreds of people and dozens of press photographers, and thousands of people followed their lead. Riots broke out everywhere.

Now the government had the perfect excuse to declare a state of emergency, putting South Africa under martial law: people could be arrested and property invaded without a warrant. Even worse, the government planned to introduce a new law banning the ANC and PAC! Now any group fighting the apartheid government was officially illegal! Just belonging to the ANC and carrying out its goals could mean **a ten-year jail sentence**!

Days later, on March 31, the treason trial was set to continue, but the key witnesses were nowhere to be found. It turned out that the night before, Nelson and his ANC colleagues **had been arrested again** in another massive police swoop that brought in an unbelievable 2,000 people! The treason trial was brought to a complete standstill.

Once again, Oliver was lucky—he'd escaped arrest—and now the ANC realized his best move was to flee the country.

The state of emergency made it practically impossible for Nelson and the lawyers to prepare the case for the defense. But eventually, the trial resumed, with Nelson and the rest of the accused appearing in court during the day and were carted back to jail at night.

On August 31, after five long months of living in horrendous prison conditions, the state of emergency was lifted. Nelson was finally allowed home to Winnie . . .

Guilty or Not Guilty?

In December 1960, Nelson and Winnie's second daughter, Zindziswa, was born. The treason trial was still rumbling on, but in early 1961 the defense hadn't even finished when the court took a six-day break, to decide on the final verdict!

Meanwhile, Nelson's bans were about to end again, and he would soon be able to leave Johannesburg freely for **the first time in five years**. The ANC knew they had to get moving with a plan, and they held an urgent meeting.

If Nelson and Winnie had been hoping for some family time together, they were about to be disappointed.

If I was found not guilty, the ANC decided I would immediately go undercover before the government could slap another charge on me.

If he was found guilty, he would be thrown in prison immediately . . . or worse! Either way, this was the last time they'd be together for a long time.

The courtroom was packed on the morning of March 29, 1961. Nelson had been on trial for a mind-numbing four years!

A rowdy crowd had managed to shove their way inside the court. The men were on pins and needles as they awaited their fate. The mood was tense as the judge read the verdict:

The accused are accordingly found not guilty and are discharged.

The men stood up and hugged one another while their supporters erupted in triumphant cheers . . .

Nelson and his colleagues marched outside, where the celebration continued. People laughed, cried, chanted, and sang. The government, however, was **less than thrilled**.

Life was not going to get any easier for Nelson and the ANC.

7 Nelson Undercover

Nelson wasted no time. Right after he was released, he spent the night in a nearby safe house. He was a free man, but in truth, now that the ANC was a banned organization, **he could be rearrested at any time**, for any ridiculous reason. Every time a car passed outside the window, he imagined the police bursting through the door. First thing the next morning, he took off.

Nelson began traveling around the country in disguise, meeting ANC officials and talking about the ANC's future plans. It wasn't easy:

Nelson Explains: Living Undercover

Your life gets turned upside down when you're living in hiding . . .

- I would keep to my hideout during the day and come out to work after dark.
- I stayed in empty apartments, on people's couches, and in servants' quarters; anywhere I could go unnoticed.
- I didn't walk as tall anymore. Instead, I spoke more softly and acted humbly. I wanted to be invisible.
- I didn't shave or cut my hair.

Life on the run was no picnic, but Nelson managed to have a little fun. The police were after him. They'd put up roadblocks throughout the country but never managed to catch him. He would appear unexpectedly as Nelson Mandela at a meeting, make a stirring speech, then quickly disappear.

He would even call newspaper reporters with false stories about the ANC's plans. That kept them off his trail!

Nelson did have a few narrow escapes, though. Once, when his car stopped at a traffic light, he realized a police chief was sitting in the car right next to him. The officer didn't spot him, but the light couldn't have changed soon enough!

Another time, he saw a Black policeman walking straight toward him. Nelson braced himself. The officer recognized him, but **he just smiled** and gave him the secret ANC salute.

Meanwhile, things were getting even worse between the government and the ANC: more raids were happening; more meetings were banned; more newspapers were shut down. And the ANC were gearing up for their most dangerous action yet . . .

The Spear of the Nation

The ANC had been against violence from the start, but now that the government had become even more strict, the organization could barely operate. If anything, they had fewer rights now than they'd had to begin with. They finally realized that if they were going to get anywhere at all **they had to become more aggressive** . . . violent even.

After many long and hard debates, they agreed a way forward. The ANC itself would remain non-violent, but Nelson would form a new separate military wing. It was called Umkhonto we Sizwe, or MK for short. And it meant "The Spear of the Nation."

Nelson had never been violent in his life, but he dived in the only way he knew how: by talking to experts and reading as much as he could.

It was agreed they would start with sabotage: by planting explosives at military bases, power plants, and railways, cutting off phone lines, etc. The ANC had made it clear that **no lives should be lost**. They just wanted to get the government to negotiate with them.

Stolen Moments

At the end of 1961, Nelson was hiding on a farm bought by an ANC supporter in the Rivonia area of Johannesburg, **disguised as a caretaker**—still named David. Dressed in his trademark overalls and cap, he was treated pretty much like a servant.

He'd prepare breakfast for the workers, run errands, and keep the place tidy. In fact, his disguise was so good that the workers never even bothered to ask him his name. They usually just called him "waiter" or "boy."

Amazingly, while Nelson was staying there, his family could visit at weekends. It was quite a feat, though, because the police were following Winnie.

Even so, Nelson cherished this time with his family—it made him feel like they were still together. But those moments were fleeting, and soon Nelson would be on the move again. Only this time, he'd be traveling much farther away.

Crossing Borders

In January 1962, Nelson had planned **an enormous secret mission** that would take him across South Africa and all over the African continent, meeting leaders and getting as much support as he could for the ANC and MK. He'd also be visiting England.

Nelson was nervous. He'd never left the country before! He couldn't get a passport (too risky for a fugitive) and had to travel on flimsy forged papers (as David Motsamayi). After a whirlwind of secret arrangements, Nelson was taken by car to neighboring Botswana, where—for the first time in his life—he hopped on a plane! Here are a few of the things he experienced:

Mbeya, Tanzania: First stop! Saw Black and white people sitting together on the hotel veranda. Shocking . . . but exciting too!
Nelson Mandela international secret agent

He'd been away for six months, and planned to end his trip in Ethiopia with another six months of military training. But, after just eight weeks, he was summoned home. Things were heating up, and the ANC needed MK's commander-in-chief back on the scene.

WANTED: NELSON MANDELA

The journey home was nerve-wracking, with abrupt changes of plan and secret border crossings to keep the police off the trail, but in late July 1962, Nelson finally arrived back on the farm in Rivonia. The next night, his ANC colleagues came to find out all about his trip—and they didn't want to see his holiday photos!

They instructed Nelson to brief the ANC's president—Chief Luthuli. But the chief lived in Durban and a trip there was **seriously risky**. The secret police knew Nelson had been out of the country illegally, and they also knew he was back. They were after him, but that didn't stop Nelson from leaving for Durban the following night, posing as a chauffeur for a white MK member named Cecil Williams.

He reached the chief and led a few more secret meetings; friends even threw him a party. It was the **first night of fun** that Nelson had had in a long time and he slept well afterward.

On Sunday, August 5, 1962, Nelson woke up ready to start his journey back to Johannesburg. He was dressed in his chauffeur disguise as usual, but Cecil took the wheel for the first leg, leaving Nelson free to daydream.

Suddenly a car flew past them. To Nelson's horror, it was filled with policemen. He turned around and saw two more cars approaching. They were instructed to pull over. For a fleeting moment, Nelson thought about escaping into the woods nearby. But **the police were armed**. He knew he wouldn't have made it.

A police officer approached and asked his name. "David Motsamayi," he answered, but the officer knew better . . .

Nelson had been on the run for nearly two years. And since the ANC and MK were considered terrorist threats, he was at the **top of the state's "most wanted" list**.

Sentenced

Nelson appeared in court a few days later, and news of his capture quickly hit the headlines.

But he breathed a sigh of relief when he heard the charges against him:

- Inciting workers to strike.
- Leaving the country without valid travel documents.

It was enough to get him locked away for ten years, but if the government had had clear evidence against MK the charges would have been much more serious—like treason (again) or sabotage.

Winnie and Nelson hadn't seen each other for months, but as he walked out of the courtroom, there she was. He gave her a huge encouraging smile. It was the best he could do because they weren't allowed anywhere near each other. He knew Winnie was going to need all the support she could get.

In November 1962, Nelson was sentenced to **five years in prison**. He'd spent four years fighting a treason case and two on the run, but now he was convicted things couldn't get any worse . . . could they?

8 Nelson Makes His Plea

In July 1963, the farm in Rivonia where Nelson had worked up many of MK's sabotage plans was raided. Walter Sisulu and other ANC leaders were arrested, and the police found a treasure trove of evidence: documents, maps, and plans—some in Nelson's handwriting. There was no getting out of this one.

Already in prison, Nelson was summoned to the prison's office and told a new charge had been brought against him: sabotage. If he was found guilty, the punishment could be **death by hanging**.

The State Vs Nelson Mandela and Others

On October 9, 1963, the biggest political trial in South Africa's history began. It was known as the Rivonia Trial.

On their first day, Nelson, Walter, and the other defendants were escorted by a heavily armed police van to the Palace of Justice, South Africa's Supreme Court. They stepped out of the van to see **hundreds of people** singing and chanting. Inside the courtroom, supporters raised their fists in solidarity.

Spectators were taking a risk just by being at the hearing. The police took their names and photographed them. In the gallery, ANC supporters rubbed shoulders with journalists from around the world.

All eleven defendants were charged with **more than 200** acts of sabotage and conspiracy to start a violent revolution.

When Nelson was asked to plead guilty or not guilty, he answered: *"My Lord, it is not I, but the government that should be in the dock. I plead not guilty."*

The other defendants followed suit. As far as they were concerned, the government had committed crimes against Black, Colored, and Indian people. They were the ones who should have been on trial!

Proceedings dragged on for six months—173 witnesses and thousands of pages of evidence were presented. The trial didn't wrap up until April 1964.

Nelson used his defense to shine a spotlight on all the injustices Black people had suffered. He explained that they'd tried peaceful protests but had been ignored. **All they'd wanted was freedom and equality for all.**

When it came to his (four-hour-long!) concluding speech, he was determined to tell the truth no matter what. As he approached his final paragraph, a hush fell upon the room. Nelson looked the judge square in the eyes and spoke these last few sentences from memory:

During my lifetime I have dedicated myself to this struggle of the African people. I have fought against white domination, and I have fought against Black domination. I have cherished the ideal of a democratic and free society in which all persons live together in harmony and with equal opportunities. It is an ideal which I hope to live for and to achieve. But if needs be, it is an ideal for which I am prepared to die.

Nelson sat down and did not look around. He could tell that **every single eye in the court was on him**. The silence seemed to last forever.

Then someone let out a sigh and the floodgates opened; African women in the courtroom wept openly.

Around the world people were moved by Nelson's speech and horror-struck by the government's appalling behavior. In places like London, people held all-night vigils to support the prisoners. Even the United Nations pleaded with the apartheid government to drop the charges and end the trial.

Nelson must have been petrified in the weeks leading up to the verdict, but you wouldn't have known it. He'd spent much of the time working toward his long-awaited LLB! That might sound strange, but trying to pass those exams stopped him from thinking about what might happen next.

In June 1964, when the time finally came for Nelson to find out his fate, the courtroom was packed with local and international press. As he entered the room, he waved to Winnie and his mother and put on a brave face. It was tough for him, but how must his mother have felt waiting to hear if her only son was about to be sentenced to death?

There was no doubt they'd be found guilty; it was **the choice of punishment** that everyone was anxious about.

Finally, the judge announced their sentence: life in prison.

Nelson looked at his fellow defendants and smiled. Had anyone ever been so happy to hear the words "life in prison"? There was a huge gasp of relief in the courtroom, but with so much support for the accused from around the world, it's likely **the judge hadn't dared go for the death penalty**.

Prisoner #466/64

On June 12, Nelson, Walter, Kathy, and the other convicted prisoners were whisked away in the dead of night to a military airport and ushered onto a plane. From the air, they could only see the rough waters of the Atlantic Ocean below. Then, in the distance, an island appeared. Robben Island. Nelson had been here before on one of his shorter stints in jail. But now, he was here to stay.

The prisoners stepped from the plane into a freezing-cold winter wind and were welcomed by a group of guards with automatic weapons. Prison wardens barked at them to strip naked and threw them some standard khaki prison uniforms. Nelson especially hated being made to wear the prison shorts.

They'd been ecstatic to escape the death penalty, but now **they faced the grim reality** of life in prison.

Gone was the constant support of their families and friends. Gone were the massive crowds that cheered them on outside the courtroom. In the isolated stone building that would be their home for who knew how long, they only had each other.

Nelson Explains: Life on Robben Island

I was 45 years old and sentenced to live here for the rest of my life.
JOHANNESBURG
ROBBEN ISLAND
CAPE TOWN
ROBBEN ISLAND PRISON

Robben Island means "Seal Island" in Dutch—it was once a haven for seals, but in 1964 it kept political prisoners away from the world. Surrounded by icy waters and high waves, the island was impossible to escape from.

My Cell

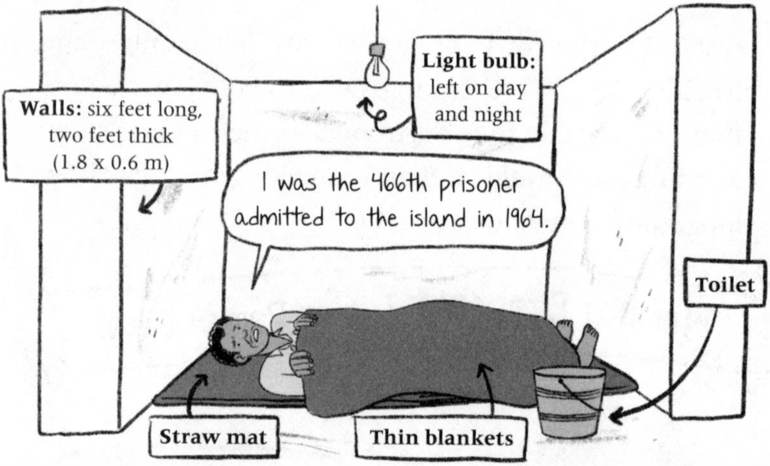

Our Grueling Schedule:

- 5:30 a.m.: A brass bell clangs.

- 6:45 a.m.: Time to empty our buckets, then eat breakfast: cornmeal porridge.

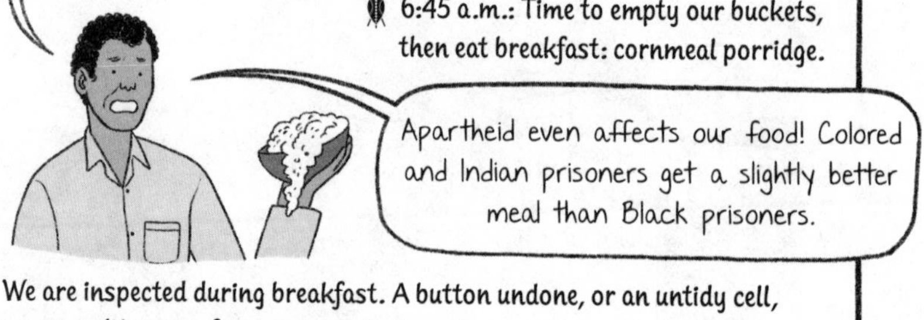

- We are inspected during breakfast. A button undone, or an untidy cell, means solitary confinement or a lost meal.
- 8 a.m. to 12 p.m.: We work in the courtyard or the quarry hammering stones, with no breaks.
- 12 p.m.: A bell rings for lunch: boiled corn for Black prisoners and corn rice—a kind of porridge—for Indian and Colored prisoners. Then it's back to work.

Life Inside

It took a few months to settle into the prison regime, and one thing that helped Nelson was exercise. He'd been a regular at his local boxing club in Johannesburg and now, each morning, he used the same training routine to keep himself fit:

- Running on the spot for 45 minutes
- 100 fingertip push-ups
- 200 sit-ups
- 50 squats

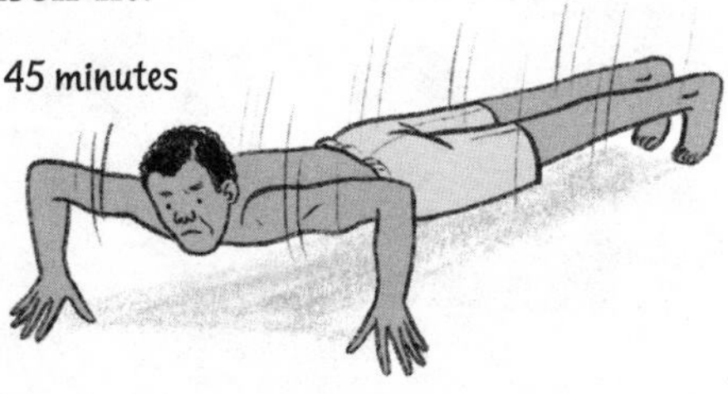

After a few months, the prisoners were allowed to take degree-level studies. Nelson threw himself into this, but he couldn't always get the texts he needed for his coursework. Books were carefully scrutinized, and any reference to current news was strictly forbidden!

We studied hard and made the most of what we had.

But nothing made up for how much Nelson missed his family. Waiting to hear from them was torture. At first, he could only have one visitor and write and receive **one letter every six months**, and the letters were so heavily censored they were often impossible to read, while the long-awaited visits only lasted thirty minutes.

Nelson was so excited when, after three months of waiting, he finally saw Winnie's beautiful face. But they were under the watchful eyes of the wardens the whole time and Nelson practically had to shout to be heard because there was a thick glass window between them.

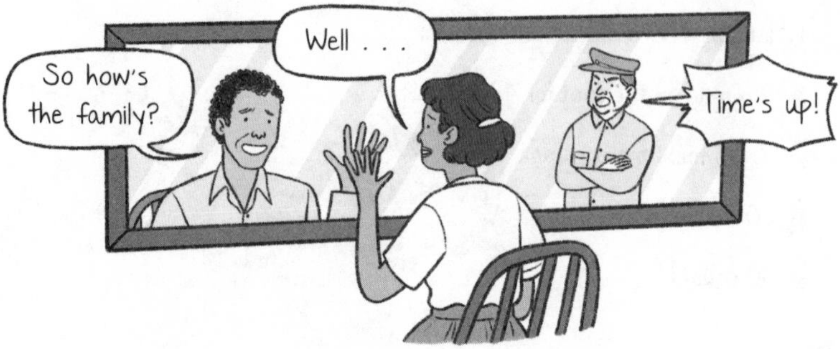

So how's the family?
Well . . .
Time's up!

How could half an hour have passed? Back in his cell Nelson went over their short conversation again and again, wanting to remember every moment. For the next few months, that visit was like a life jacket that kept Nelson afloat in stormy waters.

Nelson Explains: Communication on Robben Island

The wardens tried their best to make life difficult, but we found a few ways to outwit them!

There were rules for everything, even for visitors:

- **All conversations had to be in English or Afrikaans—so the wardens could understand them. African languages were strictly forbidden!**
- **You could only talk about family matters—no politics or the visit ended. Winnie and I invented code names for people and pretended that they were family members. When the wardens asked questions, we made up great stories.**

So who is Jumba?
Oh, he's my father's sister's daughter's brother-in-law.

And when it came to other prisoners:

- **We weren't supposed to communicate with prisoners from different sections, but we soon got around this by hiding coded messages in matchboxes and using "invisible ink."**

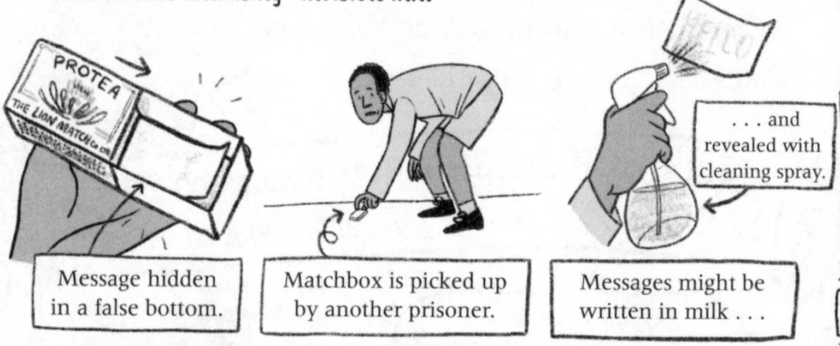

Message hidden in a false bottom.
Matchbox is picked up by another prisoner.
Messages might be written in milk . . .
. . . and revealed with cleaning spray.

Occasionally, we even got a message to the outside world with the help of a visitor or a prisoner leaving the island.

Heartbreak . . . Again

Sometimes the news the prisoners longed for was unbearably sad. Nelson's mom **only visited once**, in 1968. She seemed old, she'd lost weight, and Nelson couldn't help worrying about her.

Weeks later, a telegram came. She'd had a heart attack and died. Nelson was beside himself. He wasn't even allowed to leave prison to bury her.

I was her only son, so this was my honor and my responsibility.

Nelson's life choices were taking their toll on Winnie too. Still working for the ANC while he was in jail, she suffered bans, just like Nelson, and **she even spent some time in prison**. He agonized over her safety, but how could he help her?

Months later, in July 1969, news came that his oldest son, Thembi, had been killed in a car accident. The boy was just twenty-four years old. As their relationship had been rocky—Thembi had never really got over his parents' divorce—the news seemed all the more **unbearable**. Once again, Nelson was not allowed to attend the funeral.

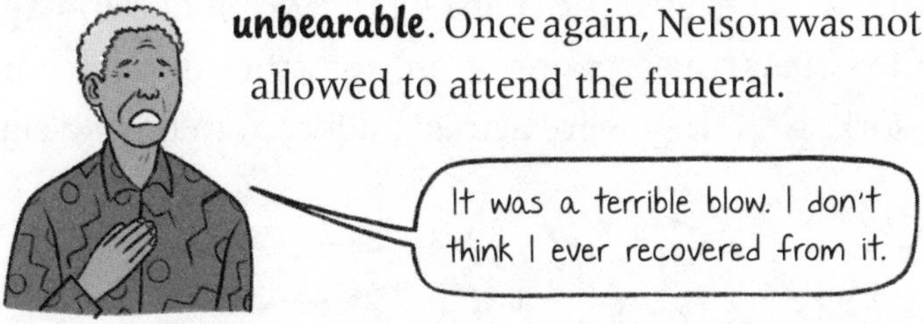

It was a terrible blow. I don't think I ever recovered from it.

Nelson felt his family's suffering and sacrifice had been far worse than his own. But as the ANC kept up the fight on the outside, inside prison Nelson channeled his sadness and frustration into a steely resolve. He'd been fighting for freedom for decades. He'd lost so much, but he wasn't going to give up now.

Changing Tides

Life on the island slowly began to improve after a new commanding officer took over the prison in the early 1970s. The prisoners managed to make friends with some of the wardens, too. It made their lives much easier. Over the years the prisoners were gradually:

- Given long pants.
- Allowed out in the courtyard at all hours during the weekend.
- Given board games and cards.
- Allowed to talk as they worked at the quarry.
- Allowed to hold meetings . . .

They formed their own little branch of the ANC and called themselves the High Organ. The men even staged **Christmas concerts** on the only day they didn't have to work. And they were actually allowed to buy sweets!

Mandela University

Their leaders might have been in prison, but freedom fighters continued to be a thorn in the side of the South

African government right into the 1970s. As more and more young men were arrested and thrown into Robben Island prison, Nelson and the others worked on a plan to keep their ANC dreams alive.

They set up a **secret university**. Turning themselves into professors, they made up their own courses, split into study groups, and lectured each other at the quarry as they worked!

The "courses" became so popular that prisoners from other sections begged to join in. Lectures had to be smuggled across to them because communication between sections was still banned.

Eager to stay busy, Nelson had also kept up with his legal work. He spent so many hours studying prisoners' cases that he might as well have been back at Mandela and Tambo! It all happened in secret, but Nelson was willing to take the risk: many of these people had been carted off to jail on **ridiculous charges** without ever catching sight of a defense lawyer.

New prisoners were helpful. They were Nelson's best news source. He would quickly tell them how things worked on Robben Island and then get down to business: How was Oliver? How were the training camps? Was MK succeeding or failing?

Nelson was working tirelessly at the fight for freedom, even behind bars. But, before he knew it, he had to somehow find more time for another secret project.

Life Story

Even outside Robben Island, information on the ANC was banned, so how could the ANC inmates get the details of their struggle to the people? Eventually someone came up with the perfect idea: Nelson should write his memoir. It would have to be top secret, of course, but a plan was quickly hatched.

- Nelson would get out of his quarry work by saying he was ill, then he'd write all night and sleep all day.

- Each day's work would be reviewed by a member of the High Organ.

- It would then be copied into a tiny shorthand manuscript to be hidden in the notebook of a prisoner who was due to be released.

Nelson started writing in 1975, the prisoner was released in 1976, but the book wasn't published until 1994!

Uprising

By the mid-1970s, everywhere in South Africa, Black people seemed to be at the end of their rope.

Nelson Explains: Johannesburg in the 1970s

Life had got worse for Black people since I'd come to Robben Island.

Most white people lived in houses like this one:

Most Black people lived in shacks like these:

Most white people had nice jobs in offices, schools, and hospitals.

Most Black people worked as servants, or worse.

Most white people were allowed to vote, and go wherever they liked.

Most Black people still couldn't vote, and their movements were still controlled by the horrendous pass laws.

However, things weren't going well for the government either. They hadn't supported education for Black people and now there was a shortage of skilled workers. Then banks and governments around the world started taking their money out of South Africa to show how much **they disapproved of apartheid**.

In June 1976, Nelson was hearing whispers of a great uprising. It had been sparked by a terrible event . . .

The Soweto Massacre

In January 1976, the South African prime minister announced that half of all high school subjects would be taught in the despised Afrikaans language (see page 10). Black teachers and students were outraged that they should have to learn and teach in a language that had been used to humiliate them. But the government didn't listen.

On June 16, 1976, about 15,000 school children gathered in Soweto for an unplanned, peaceful protest. Without any warning at all, the police opened fire on the crowd. Total chaos followed. The children fought back with sticks and stones.

At the end of the horrible tragedy, many **children were wounded and killed**. When a photograph of one of them, a thirteen-year-old boy named Hector Pieterson, was splashed across newspapers around the world, people were outraged once again. Black South Africans were furious. Riots broke out, students boycotted school, and ANC supporters protested. A whole new generation of young people were fed up and angry. They wanted freedom. Something had to change.

Light at the End of the Tunnel?

By the early 1980s, Nelson had been in prison for nearly twenty years. Here he describes some of his highs and lows:

- 1964: I was hauled off to the island (a real low).
- 1968: My fiftieth birthday (a high for the milestone, a low for the location).
- 1969–70: Found out Winnie was sentenced to 491 days in solitary confinement (a terrible low).
- 1975: My daughter Zindzi turned fifteen and made her first visit (a super high). I hadn't seen her since she was three years old!
- 1977: After thirteen years, hard labor finally ended.

Yes!

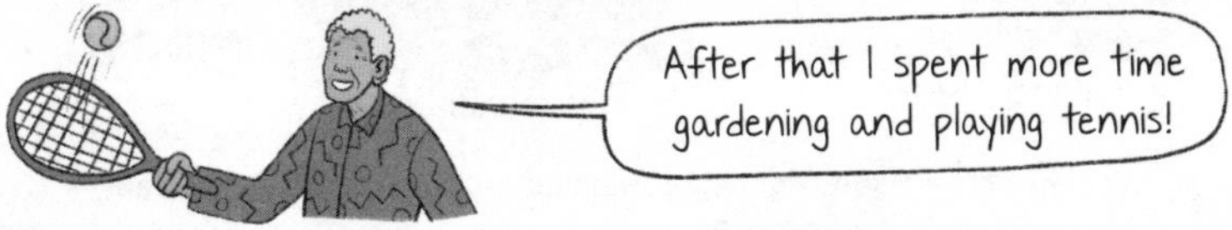

After that I spent more time gardening and playing tennis!

- 1978: My daughter Zenani visited with her newborn daughter—my grandchild!

I named her Zaziwe, which means hope. The highest of highs.

1980: We were allowed to buy newspapers (finally!).

Nelson's spirit wasn't broken. In fact, his belief in a free South Africa was stronger than ever. As things got worse in the country, thanks to plays and protest songs, Nelson's larger-than-life reputation as a freedom fighter grew, even though he was still behind bars. Outside of South Africa, his star was beginning to rise too . . .

FREE NELSON MANDELA

Around the world, people didn't know the name Nelson Mandela until a Black South African newspaper launched a campaign to release him in 1980. Oliver Tambo, now head of the ANC, had suggested putting a face to the struggle, and Nelson's had been chosen.

The Free Nelson Mandela campaign gradually picked up steam, and by the middle of the 1980s support stretched from the US to Chile and India.

Nelson was flooded with honors—gardens, parks, and streets around the world were named after him. He even influenced scientists:

I name this nuclear particle the Mandela Particle.
Nice one!

More than 20,000 government officials from cities in every corner of the world signed a declaration demanding that Nelson be freed. Nelson Mandela was suddenly a household name.

On March 31, 1982, sixty-three-year-old Nelson got the shock of his life when some prison officials marched into his cell and told him to pack his bags. They didn't say why.

With no chance to say goodbye to the friends who had helped him survive those grueling years, Nelson and three other prisoners were shuttled out of the prison and onto a ferry to Cape Town.

As he watched the island disappear from sight, Nelson actually **felt a bit nostalgic**. He'd kind of got used to Robben Island. And where he was heading now was anybody's guess.

9 Nelson Casts His First Vote

The four prisoners had, in fact, been taken from one prison just to be dropped into another one, called Pollsmoor. There was a difference, though . . .

The men were given their own space on the top floor of the prison and they now had:

- **Clean, modern rooms; a flushing toilet; a sink; and two showers.**
- **Real beds with mattresses and sheets.**
- **Towels!**

- **No more cornmeal—three meals a day with vegetables and meat!**

Nelson welcomed the change, but it still sent his head spinning. The four men had no idea why they'd been transferred, but they didn't let that stop them enjoying the new place. To the frustration of his roommates, however, Nelson kept up his early-morning exercise routine.

Give it a rest, Nelson.

UNBELIEVABLE

Visits at Pollsmoor were a breath of fresh air. After 1984, Nelson was actually allowed to be in the same room as his visitor, with no divider. He hadn't so much as held Winnie's hand for an unbelievable twenty-one years, so that first time the two of them were able to touch each other, Nelson held on like he would never let go.

Outside Pollsmoor, though, the violence was getting worse. The South African army had launched raids on ANC offices and **members of MK were being executed**. And they were retaliating with explosives—targeting the South African military. The ANC hoped that if the country was ungovernable they'd topple the government by force. Life for Black people in South Africa was still miserable, but the whole world was watching.

Nelson Explains: Apartheid and the Rest of the World

I could hardly believe what I was reading in the papers.

News spread so much faster in the 1980s. More homes around the world had TVs, and when viewers saw what was happening to Black people in South Africa, they demanded change.

Anti-apartheid groups were popping up all over the world, and citizens were protesting in their thousands.

Countries pulled their ambassadors out of South Africa. Banks stopped lending South Africa money.

Twenty years earlier I'd asked for economic sanctions (stopping trade or business relationships with South Africa). Now sanctions were actually happening. With so much pressure on the economy, the government might really be forced to change.

The US Congress had even passed an anti-apartheid law, making it illegal for many US companies to do business with South Africa.

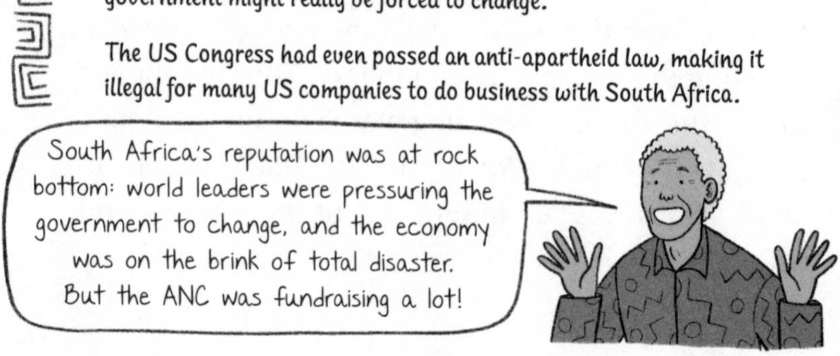

South Africa's reputation was at rock bottom: world leaders were pressuring the government to change, and the economy was on the brink of total disaster. But the ANC was fundraising a lot!

Nelson knew something had to be done. He started to think about talking to the enemy—the government! But the idea seemed so absurd that he didn't dare tell anyone at first. Not the ANC. Not his cellmates. Not even Winnie.

The government had been testing the waters too. The ANC was still banned but they'd been watching Nelson's international popularity grow, and they knew if they wanted peace, **he was the man to talk to**. On January 31, 1985, the government boldly offered Nelson his freedom . . . he'd just have to agree to one thing: to reject the violence of his organization.

Nelson said no. He'd never really approved of violence, but if he left prison without the government making any improvements for Black people, nothing would have changed. He'd have to get involved in the struggle all over again. But at least the government had made an offer. A door was slowly opening . . .

Inside Pollsmoor, conditions began to get even better for Nelson. He got his own room, so he could start organizing things in secret. Cautiously, he wrote letters to government officials asking for meetings.

If the talks were a spectacular disaster, the ANC wouldn't be to blame. They could say this old man went off his rocker.

When a group of heads of state decided to visit South Africa on a fact-finding mission—to see just how bad things were in the country—they asked to see Nelson too.

The meeting was a pretty big deal, and the government was eager to make a good impression. Even so, the day before, Nelson was surprised when a tailor showed up at his room to fit him for a suit.

Ha, ha, Nelson, I almost mistook you for the prime minister!

Early the next morning, Nelson slipped into a pinstriped suit that fit him like a glove.

He was finally ready.

Talking to the Enemy

Meanwhile, the country was still struggling. Any criticism of the government was now illegal, and the police could use **extreme force** to try to control protests. Change was desperately needed, but progress was slow—Nelson and the government were talking, but those talks would take one step forward and then two steps back . . . Finally, in 1987, the government made its first real proposal.

They promised a small committee would start serious private discussions with Nelson. They even agreed to Nelson's conditions.

One day, in December 1988, Nelson was suddenly told to pack his bags. He was on the move again.

About an hour later, Nelson arrived at another prison: Victor Verster, near Cape Town. His car drove past some trees and stopped in front of a cottage surrounded by a concrete wall.

I couldn't have designed it better myself!

The cottage was Nelson's new "prison cell," complete with **a lounge, a large kitchen, and a bedroom**. He was surprised, but then, he'd made some progress with the talks, and international pressure was crushing the country. He knew it was only a matter of time before a deal was made.

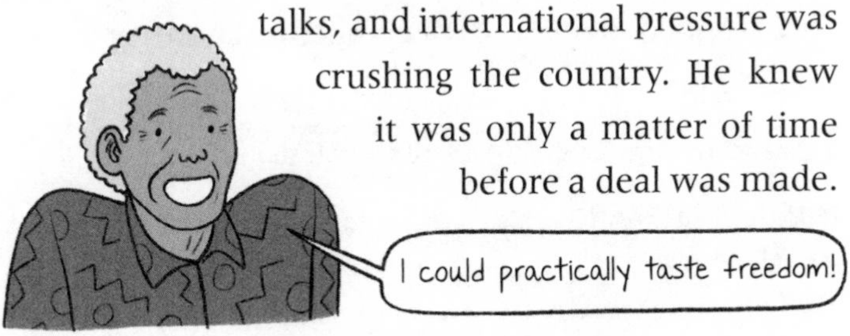

I could practically taste freedom!

The next morning, Nelson took another spin around his new home, and discovered it was even fancier than he'd thought . . . more bedrooms . . . a pool . . . Nelson even had his own private chef!

I'll dry.
That's my job, Nelson. Will you please sit down?

On his seventy-first birthday, the following July, Nelson threw **a huge family party**. Having his wife and children in the same place at the same time was the best present, and he'd been in prison so long that his children now had quite a few children of their own! For the first time, the family party included his grandchildren too.

While his chef prepared a feast, the adults chatted away and the kids played and watched TV. It was almost like Nelson was living a normal life . . .

But the discussions with the government started and stopped over and over again. There were two sticking points:

1. The government wanted the armed struggle to end.

2. Nelson and the ANC wanted everyone to have the same freedoms and the right to vote.

Unexpectedly, in August 1989, a new president, F. W. de Klerk, was sworn in and things picked up the pace. Soon after, eight of Nelson's old Robben Island comrades were released with no restrictions and no bans. They'd be able to shout the words "Mandela" and "ANC" from the rooftops (if they wanted to) and the police wouldn't arrest them.

From that moment on, South Africa's new president started **taking apart the whole awful apartheid system** brick by brick. He unbanned the ANC and other anti-apartheid organizations, put a stop to executions, and the two sides were able to reach an agreement at last.

The moment the world (and Nelson) had been waiting for finally came during a live press conference in February 1990:

I am now in a position to announce that Mr. Nelson Mandela will be released.

After twenty-seven years in prison, when he was seventy-one, Nelson would finally be free.

Free at Last

On February 11, 1990, while Nelson woke up in his comfortable prison cottage for the last time, millions of people in South Africa and around the world were desperate to catch a glimpse of him for the first time.

But Nelson wasn't even thinking about his freedom. The house was buzzing with activity. **He did his exercises**, had a medical check-up, had to call the ANC—and there was a speech to finish too.

There was barely time to say goodbye and thank the people who'd looked after him, before he was rushed into a car with Winnie and driven to the gates of the prison. But just before they got there, the car stopped so Winnie and Nelson could get out and walk toward the jubilant crowds.

It was another moment the world had been waiting for. But it came as a shock to Nelson:

Cameras were clicking and reporters were shouting questions Nelson could barely pick out. ANC supporters were cheering at the tops of their lungs. It was **absolute chaos**.

When a strange object was thrust in his face, Nelson jumped back, startled. Winnie had to explain that it was a microphone!

Nelson soon found his footing. He took a few steps forward—his first real steps of freedom—and raised his right fist in the air. The crowd gave a thunderous roar. And suddenly, Nelson felt strong, confident, and happy. But he was totally unprepared for what would greet him on the other side of those prison gates.

Global Hero

In those first few weeks of freedom, **thousands upon thousands** of people showed up wherever Nelson was speaking. They couldn't get enough of the leader who'd sacrificed his life for a free South Africa.

Even his Soweto home was surrounded by throngs of people. They sang. They danced. They cheered. And they stayed . . . for days . . . weeks . . . months. Nelson began to see just how much he meant to the people. All he could do was give himself to them. Once again, it would be his family who paid the price.

With his popularity soaring, the ANC didn't want to

lose momentum, and Nelson was quickly whisked off on an international tour, meeting world leaders and celebrities, attending fancy private dinners, speaking to unbelievably huge crowds, and sharing his story with the world:

In Cairo he was jostled by a mob, he lost a shoe . . . and his wife!

In London a concert was given in his honor at Wembley Stadium.

In Paris, the French president, François Mitterrand, treated him like royalty.

In New York City, one million people attended a parade.

The tour worked. Money rolled in to the ANC's coffers from VIPs, celebrities, and ordinary people. Nelson Mandela was a global hero.

The Darkest Hour

In South Africa, however, things were still not improving. The death toll from raids and riots had skyrocketed, and though swift changes were needed, the talks dragged on and on.

Even at home, Nelson had to admit that his marriage with Winnie was crumbling. She'd fought tirelessly for his freedom while Nelson was in prison, but their paths had split along the way. Nelson wanted to include white people in his plans for the country; Winnie didn't agree. While Nelson had built a reputation as a peacemaker, Winnie had built a reputation as troublemaker. She'd been caught up in some scandals and was tried and found guilty of kidnapping!

Nelson had been elected president of the ANC a year earlier and the news of his wife's behavior was just too much. So, on April 13, 1992, Nelson announced **he and Winnie were separating**. The marriage had survived his twenty-seven-year jail sentence, but only two years of freedom.

There was more bad news to come.

In 1993, Oliver Tambo had a sudden stroke and died.

Nelson was bereft. The two of them had been partners in law and in politics. Oliver had achieved so much for the ANC, leading them from abroad for twenty-four years. He'd seen Nelson released, but he'd never had the chance to vote in his own country. Now Nelson was more determined than ever to do something about that.

Breakthrough

Negotiations with the government continued, but times were tough. When one of the ANC's most popular leaders, Chris Hani, was assassinated in April 1993, Nelson's leadership was put to the test. South Africa was on the brink of civil war, and Nelson was asked to address the country on national TV.

Luckily, his appeal for peace worked, and over the next few months, **real change started to happen without violence**. In June 1993, the ANC and the government finally agreed on a date for South Africa's first national election where all races could vote: April 27, 1994.

It was fantastic news, but the campaign wasn't going to be easy. The ANC had been a movement. Now they had to become a political party. As president of the ANC, Nelson was their candidate for president of South Africa, and he hit the ground running, crisscrossing the country like it was the old days (only now he wasn't driving but being driven!), listening to the hopes and fears and complaints of the people. He asked them to be patient.

Although it may seem unfair, be patient. You won't all be driving fancy cars and swimming in your own pools any time soon. Change is going to come slowly.
Just some running water would be nice.

He encouraged them to vote and work hard. Nelson loved these rallies. He felt at home with the people.

When Nelson **won the Nobel Peace Prize** with President de Klerk in December 1993, it was further proof the he'd done the right thing.

Election Day at Last!

People walked miles and waited hours for the polling stations to open on April 27. Nelson had waited a long time too! As he approached the polling station, he was deep in thought, remembering all the people who'd helped him over the years but had never had a chance to vote themselves. After five decades of struggle and so much unbearable personal loss, now, here he was, **about to cast his first vote**.

It took days to count the votes, but the ANC were the clear winners, so on the day of Nelson's first vote, he also became South Africa's first Black president.

People danced in the streets as international congratulations streamed in. At the ANC victory bash that evening, Nelson spoke to an electrified crowd, his heart full of pride and joy and love. They were now free at last, and it was his true honor to serve the people. But after all the feel-good speeches and photos and handshakes and hugs, a new South Africa had to be built. And Nelson already had his sleeves rolled up.

Father of the Nation

White South Africans must've been nervous about the future. Their government hadn't exactly been fair when they'd held the reins. But **Nelson wasn't looking for revenge**. He knew that for South Africa's economy to recover, everyone—people of all races—needed to work together.

He kept on white staff who had been employed by the previous government. Both national anthems ("Nkosi Sikelel' iAfrika" for Black people and "Die Stem" for white people) played at his inauguration. He even read an Afrikaans poem in parliament.

And when South Africa hosted and won the 1995 Rugby World Cup, he wore the green-and-gold jersey of South Africa's mostly white rugby team—not all Black people were happy about that, but it helped white people to feel he was on their side too.

Bringing the people together wasn't always easy. When Nelson set up a truth and reconciliation commission that could **pardon people accused of terrible crimes during apartheid**, many Black people were enraged. It was just like pouring salt on a wound.

One of the most incredible things Nelson achieved as president, however, was something he'd dreamed of for decades. In 1996, having brought politicians and freedom fighters together to help write it, he presented a new constitution.

South Africa's World-Famous Constitution

- It gave most importance to: human dignity, human equality, and human rights and freedoms.
- It shunned: racism, sexism, and any other form of discrimination.

One Harvard University lawyer described it as:

The most admirable constitution in the history of the world.

All Good Things Come to an End

After all those years of struggle, by 1999 he must have been very, very tired, but Nelson still had a lot to live for. A few years earlier, at the age of seventy-five, **he'd fallen in love again** with Graça Machel, a rights campaigner for women and children. She'd also been a politician and first lady of Mozambique, but she was reluctant to get involved with Nelson at first. Then, on his eightieth birthday, she gave him the best possible present: she married him. And now he definitely planned to spend his last years peacefully with his new wife, his children, and his many grand- and great-grandchildren.

Nelson might have given up politics, but with Graça by his side, he carried on working for good causes, helping to draw up a peace agreement in Burundi after seven years of civil war and establishing the Nelson Mandela Foundation to keep alive his ideas about freedom and equality for all long after his own death.

In 2004, he finally stepped down from public life.

Nelson never turned his back on the struggle for freedom and equality—not in the twenty-seven years he'd toiled away in prison, not in the four years that he'd pleaded for free and fair elections, not in the five years that he honorably served as South Africa's president.

By fighting for freedom in his country, Nelson showed the whole world the power that **a single person** has to spark change.

EPILOGUE

Nelson might have retired, but people still couldn't get enough of him.

His ninetieth birthday celebrations in 2008 lasted **an entire year**! There were exhibitions, stamps, and gold coins created in his honor, and a huge concert was held for him in Hyde Park, London, hosted by Hollywood megastar Will Smith.

But the main event was a huge bash in Qunu, with his family, friends, and a whopping 500 other guests! Shortly after his release in 1990, Nelson had gone back to Qunu to pay his respects at his mom's grave and soak up all the sights of his childhood. Lots of things in the village had changed, but lots had stayed the same. People were still living in mud huts, without electricity or water, but now, instead of the clear streams, green grass, and tidy homesteads of his childhood, there was trash everywhere and the compounds were shabby. That visit had reminded Nelson how much work still had to be done to give everyone a fair chance at life.

After the fanfare of his ninetieth birthday, Nelson had a few more good years—his face was even printed on a new set of banknotes.

Now they'll never get rid of me!

And then the man who'd fought his whole life fell ill and could fight no more. Nelson died of an infection on December 5, 2013. He was ninety-five.

Around the world, people mourned the loss of a great leader and true hero. Thousands attended his memorial in South Africa. Heads of state and foreign dignitaries paid their respects. Then US president Barack Obama gave a stirring speech about how much Nelson meant to him and to the world.

Maybe his father was onto something when he named him Rolihlahla, or "troublemaker." Nelson had stirred up **a heck of a lot** of trouble to bring peace and equality to his country. He was a troublemaker who changed the world.

Well, I am not a saint, unless you think of a saint as a sinner who keeps on trying.

Pronunciation Guide

Check this list to find out how we say some of the words and names in this book. Many of them are in isiXhosa, one of South Africa's official languages.

IsiXhosa includes some click sounds when certain letters are used.

"X" is pronounced with a click that comes from the side of the mouth. Open your mouth wide, keep your tongue on the roof of your mouth, and make a sound like horses' hooves.

"Q" has the tongue up in the roof of the mouth. Pull the tongue and jaw down to make a knocking sound.

These sounds are then combined with the five vowels: a, e, i, o, u.

Word/Name	Explanation	Pronunciation	Meaning
amandla	An ANC supporters' cry.	a-mand-lah	power
Garlick **Mbekeni**	Nelson's cousin.	Mh-beh-ke-nee	place/put
Graça **Machel**	Nelson's third wife.	Grassa Mashel	
isiXhosa	The Xhosa people's native language.	e-see-Xho-sa Use the X-click sound for "Xho."	
Jongintaba Dalindyebo	The Thembu regent and Nelson's guardian.	Jaw-ngih-ntah-bah Da-lee-n-dee-yeh-bo	one who looks upon the mountain
Madiba	Nelson's clan name.	Ma-dee-ba	
Madiba **Thembekile**	Nelson's oldest child (a son).	Tem-beh-key-leh	trustworthy
Makaziwe	Nelson's first daughter, who died, and his second daughter, who survived.	Mah-ka-zee-way	may she be known
Makgatho Lewanika	Nelson and Evelyn's third child (a son).	Mah-kgah-toe	ways (from the Zulu language)
Mbashe River	A river running through Eastern Cape province.	Mbah-sha-e	

Mbekela	The brothers who suggested Nelson should go to school.	Mm-beh-keh-lah	
Ngangelizwe	Thembu chief.	Ngah-ngeh-lee-zwee	
ngawethu	ANC supporters' answer to the cry *"Amandla!"*	ngah-we-tu	It shall be ours!
Ngubengcuka	A Thembu king and Nelson's great-grandfather.	N-goo-ben-g-soo-krr	blanket of a wolf
Nkosikazi No-England	Jongintaba's wife.	Nko-see-ka-zee	wife
Nomafu	Jongintaba's daughter.	No-mah-foo	clouds
Nomzamo Winnie **Madikizela**	Mandela's second wife.	Nom-zah-mo Ma-dee-kee-zela	tries her best
Nxeko	The brother of Sabata and Jongintaba.	N-x-eco Use the X-click sound.	
Phathiwe	Nelson's aunt.	Pah-tee-way	carried/handled
Qunu	The village where Nelson grew up.	Q-oon-u Use the Q-click sound.	
Rolihlahla	The name Nelson was given when he was born.	Rhholi-lla-lla To say "Rhholi," keep your tongue at the back of your mouth and make a "Rhrr" sound. For "lla" put your tongue on the roof of your mouth and pull it down, keeping your mouth wide.	tree-shaker/ troublemaker
Sabata	Brother of Jongintaba, he became the Thembu king and ruled until 1986.	Sah-bar-tar	
Thembu	One of Nelson's clan names (a family can have several different clan names).	Teh-m-buh	
Xhosa	An ethnic group of southern African people whose homeland is now in the Eastern Cape province.	Xho-sa Use the X-click for "Xho."	
Zenani	Nelson and Winnie's older daughter.	Ze-nah-nee	What have you brought into the world?
Zindziswa	Nelson and Winnie's younger daughter.	Zee-ndsi-swa	firm, steadfast, not easily shaken

Timeline

July 18, 1918
Nelson is born and given the name Rolihlahla.

1930
Nelson's father dies, and he is adopted by the regent, Jongintaba.

1938
Nelson finishes school and starts studying at the University of Fort Hare.

1939
Nelson and his best friend, Justice, run away to Johannesburg.

1942
Nelson starts work at a law firm in Johannesburg and completes his degree.

1943
Nelson enrolls at the University of the Witwatersrand.

1944
Nelson becomes an active member of the ANC and helps form their Youth League.

Nelson marries Evelyn Mase.

1946
Nelson and Evelyn's first child, Madiba Thembekile, is born.

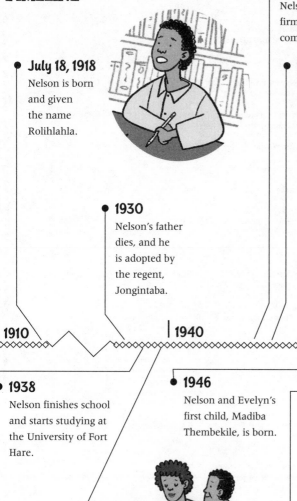

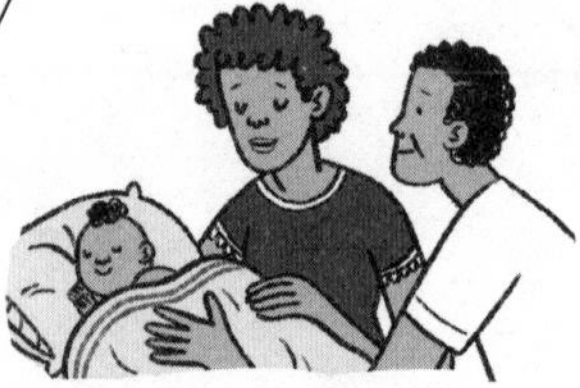

1947
Evelyn gives birth to a daughter, Makaziwe, but, sadly, she dies at just nine months old.

Nelson becomes leader of his local branch of the ANC.

1948
The National Party are elected to govern South Africa; their policies are based on a racist system called apartheid.

1910 | 1940 | 1945

1952

Nelson and the ANC start planning a national Defiance Campaign against the government.

June 26, 1952

Nelson is arrested during the campaign and spends two days in prison.

July 1952

Nelson is charged with violation of the Suppression of Communism Act, and banned from leaving Johannesburg for six months.

Nelson and Oliver Tambo open South Africa's first-ever Black law firm.

1953

Nelson and Evelyn have another daughter and name her Makaziwe, after the baby they lost.

1955

Nelson and the ANC draw up a Freedom Charter for an equal South Africa.

LIBÉREZ MANDELA
BOJKOTTA SYDAFRIKA

1956

Nelson is arrested for high treason. He and his ANC colleagues are confined in Johannesburg Prison for two weeks and a long pre-trial begins.

Evelyn leaves Nelson and takes their children with her.

1950 | 1955 | 1960

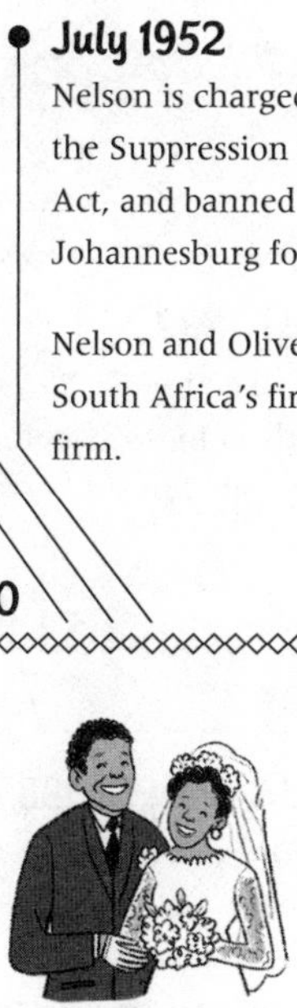

June 26, 1950

Nelson helps plan the National Day of Protest against apartheid and police brutality.

1950

Nelson and Evelyn's second son, Makgatho Lewanika, is born.

1958

Nelson marries Nomzamo Winifred Madikizela.

1959

Nelson and Winnie's first child, Zenani, is born.

1960

Nelson and Winnie's second daughter, Zindziswa, is born.

March 29, 1961

After a four-year trial, Nelson and the ANC are found not guilty of high treason.

1961

Nelson goes on the run. He forms a new military wing of the (now illegal) ANC: Umkhonto we Sizwe (the MK).

January 1962
Nelson begins his international secret mission to get support for the ANC and MK.

August 5, 1962
Nelson is captured by the police.

1964
Nelson is found guilty and sentenced to life in prison on Robben Island.

1969
Nelson's son Thembi is killed in a car accident at age twenty-four.

1976
Nelson begins writing his memoir.

Many children are killed during the Soweto Massacre.

March 31, 1982
Nelson is taken from Robben Island to Pollsmoor Prison, in Cape Town.

1965 | 1980 | 1985

October 9, 1963
The Rivonia Trial begins. Nelson is charged with inciting workers to strike, illegally leaving the country and sabotage.

1980
The Free Nelson Mandela campaign begins, gaining international support.

January 31, 1985
The government offers Nelson his freedom in return for rejecting the violence of the ANC. Nelson refuses.

November 1962
He is sentenced to five years in prison.

1987
Nelson begins meeting with government officials to discuss equality.

Nelson, you can go home!

1988
Nelson moves to Victor Verster Prison—where his prison cell is a cottage.

1989
F. W. de Klerk becomes president of South Africa.

February 11, 1990
Nelson is finally set free.

1990
He begins an international tour, sharing his story with the world.

Winnie?
Nelson!

1992
Nelson and Winnie announce their separation.

1993
Nelson and President de Klerk jointly win the Nobel Peace Prize.

1994
His memoir, *Long Walk to Freedom,* is published.

April 27, 1994
Nelson is elected president in the first South African election in which all races can vote.

1996
Nelson presents a new South African constitution, promoting equality and freedom for all.

1998
Nelson marries Graça Machel.

1999
Nelson establishes the Nelson Mandela Foundation. He ends his five-year term as president.

2008
Nelson's ninetieth birthday celebrations span a whole year!

December 5, 2013
Nelson dies.

1990 | 1995 | 2010

Glossary

accession: Gaining a position of power.

Allies: The group of countries that fought alongside Britain during the two world wars.

ANC: African National Congress

ancestor/s: Members of a family stretching back over time.

boycott: To refuse to go to, use, or buy something as part of a protest.

censor: To remove undesirable content from a letter, book, movie, or other material.

chauffeur: Someone who is employed to drive a private car.

civil war: A war where both sides are from the same country.

clan: A group of people who share the same ancestors.

colony: A place occupied and controlled by people from another country.

conquer: To overcome or take by force.

constitution: Basic principles that influence the way a country is governed.

custom: A way of acting that is usual for a person or group—like a tradition.

democracy: A system of government that allows all citizens to vote and elect representatives into power.

exile: The punishment of being sent away from your country and not allowed to return.

expulsion: To be expelled or forced to leave.

fable: A short story that teaches a message about how to behave.

fellowship: Company and friendship.

flogging: Beating harshly with a whip or stick.

fugitive: Someone who is in hiding.

guardian: An adult with a legal responsibility for a child.

homestead: Collection of huts housing one family or group.

inmate: Prisoner.

LLB : Bachelor of law degree.

magistrate: Judge.

massacre: The killing of a large

number of people in a particularly cruel or violent way.

memoir: A life story.

missionary: Someone who works for a church visiting countries around the world, to teach or convert people to their religion.

MK (Umkonto we Sizwe): The Spear of the Nation—the military wing of the ANC.

privilege: A benefit only given to certain groups of people.

prosecutor: A lawyer who tries to prove that someone accused of a crime is guilty.

ransack: Search a place thoroughly and often roughly.

reconciliation: Agreement or forgiveness after a disagreement.

recruit: Get someone to join an organization or cause.

regent: Someone appointed leader while the actual ruler is too young to take on the role.

resign: Give up a job or duty.

rural: To do with the countryside.

sabotage: Deliberately damage or destroy something, usually for political reasons.

sit-in: Refusing to leave a place in protest against the way it is organized, for example, if it is a racially segregated area.

solidarity: When a group of people share common goals or ideas.

solitary confinement: Punishing a prisoner by keeping them alone in a cell away from other prisoners.

treason: Betraying your country or ruler by going to war against it or giving sensitive information to its enemy.

tribe: A group of people who share the same language, social traditions, and ancestors.

vigil: To stay awake overnight in order to support a cause.

violation: Not following a rule.

Education is a powerful weapon.

Notes

107 "My Lord . . . not guilty." Nelson Mandela, *Long Walk to Freedom: The Autobiography of Nelson Mandela,* page 355.

108 "During my lifetime . . . prepared to die." Mandela, *Long Walk to Freedom,* page 368.

133 "I am now . . . will be released." President F. W. de Klerk, "News Session on Mandela" (speech).

142 "The most . . . of the world." Mark S. Kende. *Comparative Constitutional Law South African Cases and Materials in a Global Context.* 2015, page xxi.

145 "Well, I am . . . keeps on trying." Matthew Dowd, "Nelson Mandela: Maybe Not a Saint, But He Kept on Trying and Gave Us All He Had."

Bibliography

Cowell, Alan. "Mandela Celebrates His 90th Birthday." *New York Times,* July 19, 2008. See nytimes.com/2008/07/19/world/africa/19mandela.html.

de Klerk, President F. W. "News Session on Mandela" (speech). *New York Times,* February 11, 1990. See nytimes.com/1990/02/11/world/south-africa-s-new-era-transcript-of-de-klerk-s-news-session-on-mandela.html.

Dowd, Matthew. "Nelson Mandela: Maybe Not a Saint, But He Kept on Trying and Gave Us All He Had." *ABC News.* See abcnews.go.com/International/nelson-mandela-saint-gave-us/story?id=19369750.

"A History of Apartheid in South Africa South African History Online (SAHO). See sahistory.org.za/article/history-apartheid-south-africa.

Kende, Mark S. *Comparative Constitutional Law South African Cases and Materials in a Global Context.* Durham, North Carolina: Carolina Academic Press, 2015.

"Mandela Archives." Nelson Mandela Foundation. Nelsonmandela.org.

Mandela, Nelson. *Long Walk to Freedom: The Autobiography of Nelson Mandela.* New York: Back Bay Books, 1995.

"Nelson Rolihlahla Mandela." South African History Online (SAHO). See sahistory.org.za/people/nelson-rolihlahla-mandela.

INDEX

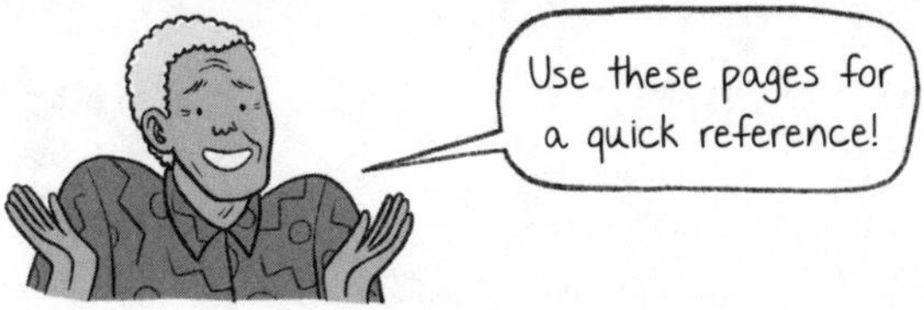
Use these pages for a quick reference!

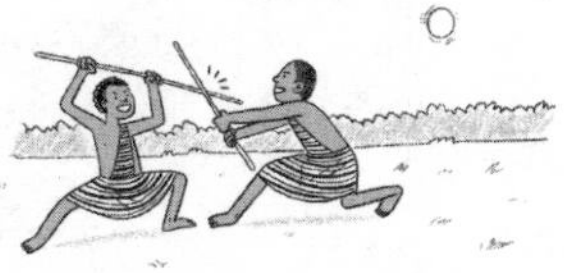